To Dad
Happy Christmas 1981
love
Linda, Geoff, Carol
& Matthew
+ x x x

"HURRICANE" HIGGINS' SNOOKER SCRAPBOOK

ACKNOWLEDGEMENTS

The authors gratefully acknowledge permission for the use of photographs in this book from

Cue World
Daily Mirror
Sunday People
Guernsey Press Company
Marcus of Mayfair
Belfast Telegraph
Express Newspapers
Manchester Evening News
Dave Muscroft
Allsport Photographic
Hy Money

We would like to make particular acknowledgement to Vince Laverty of Cue World for his generous help.

We would also like to express our grateful thanks to all those players who have allowed us to include their thoughts and comments in the book.

All care and attention has been taken in the effort to trace the copyright holders of photographs included.

We apologise to any photographer we were unable to identify.

"HURRICANE" HIGGINS' SNOOKER SCRAPBOOK

Alex Higgins
with
Angela Patmore

**PICTORIAL
PRESENTATIONS**

SOUVENIR PRESS

First published 1981 by Souvenir Press Ltd,
43 Great Russell Street, London WC1B 3PA
and simultaneously in Canada

Reprinted May 1981

ISBN 0 285 62486 5 Case bound
ISBN 0 285 62485 7 Paperback

Filmset and printed in Great Britain by
BAS Printers Limited, Over Wallop, Hampshire

CONTENTS

The Jampot 6
Eddie Charlton 11
Fred Davis 13
Stables to Tables 14
Steve Davis 17
Patsy Fagan 19
Back to Belfast 21
Terry Griffiths 27
Perrie Mans 30
The Year of the Hurricane 31
Tony Meo 34
Doug Mountjoy 36
The Big Match 37
John Pulman 41
Ray Reardon 44
Trouble 49
John Spencer 54
More Trouble 56
Kirk Stevens 61
David Taylor 62
Turning the Corner 63
Dennis Taylor 67
Jack Rea 70
Cliff Thorburn 71
Willie Thorne 73
Fits and Starts 74
John Virgo 86
Jimmy White 88
Rex Williams 90
Almost There 92
Graham Miles 114
Jim Wych 117
Future Higgins 121

THE JAMPOT

WHEN I was eleven, a gipsy came to the front door of our council house in Abingdon Street, Belfast, totting for old clothes. Our Mum, being the sort who would never turn anybody away, invited her in for a cup of tea. She should have said a cup of tea-leaves, because this gipsy turned out to be a fortune-teller. 'There's going to be a star in the family,' she said, and immediately our Mum cast her mind round to one of my three sisters, Ann, who sang. She'd actually won talent competitions: Belfast's answer to Connie Francis. In fact, she still sings, when she isn't running her own hairdressing business. 'It's not a girl,' said the gipsy. 'It's a little boy.' At the time of the incident, I do believe I was round the corner in a billiard hall off the Donegall Road called the Jampot. That was the official name of it. Teachers at Kelvin School used to call it the Gluepot, because they could never get me out.

(Playwright Stewart Love, Alex's maths teacher: I remember Alex quite well. He was remarkable for his absence. We heard rumours at the school that there was this wee boy who was a phenomenal snooker player. We didn't realize it was him. We used to have a small billiard table in the staff room, and he went so far as to ask us if he could practise on it in the lunch hours. We wouldn't let him, so we were never to see Alex Higgins give an exhibition in Kelvin School staff room. He was 14 then, and a very bright and pleasant wee fellow: I liked him. But school took second place I'm afraid. Snooker was the main priority.)

Perhaps I didn't study that much in school. I wish I had done now, because I think there might have been something there, but then I wasn't the only one. A lot of us pupils were stuck in that Gluepot—sometimes the whole class. I don't think it's necessarily a bad thing: kids are better off in a snooker hall than running about vandalizing tower blocks. Eddie Charlton has introduced snooker into Australian schools now, and they've accepted it because snooker's a good sport, a decent sport. It keeps people out of trouble. Well, it keeps *most* people out of trouble.

I was in the Jampot morning, noon and night, trying to hustle grown men. I'd never play boys my own age. I used to put my school-bag under the table, away from the roving eyes of truant officers. It was hard, too, because you'd spend the best part of your time marking for players who were good. You'd go in there with your pocket-money, 2/6 or 50p or whatever it was, and lose it. I was a kid, but they'd take my money, no qualms. And then you'd to stand there for an hour-and-a-half or two hours marking the scores down. Each player in turn, if he won, was supposed to give you threepence. But some people were mean and they wouldn't give you threepence, they'd give you a penny. So you'd mark for a long time before you could build up your bank and go back into the game. You might be boiling inside, waiting to play, and there you'd be, scribbling on the back of a cigarette packet. Still, it was a good way to learn. I was watching their mistakes. I was taking it all in.

All my money went on snooker. I used to look forward to visiting aunts and uncles in the Shankhill Road, because you never knew, but they might give you a couple of bob. My Mum used to give me sixpence dinner money. You can guess what I did with that, as well. Eventually, in the evening one of my sisters would be sent to fetch me out, as I'd no food inside me, except maybe a Mars bar.

Jean and 'Sandy'—sister and brother at a tender age.

6

The King, aged three, on the occasion of the Queen's Coronation (and mine). 'Royal Family': left to right: my sister Ann, friend Carol, sister Jean, me.

Same scene—myself in centre.

(Anne Brown, Alex's sister: It got so that I'd to chase after him with his dinner. He wouldn't sit. He'd 36 days at school in his last year: the rest of the time he was in the Jampot. I don't think there was any way you could have stopped him once he got out of the house.)

Ann or Isobel would open the big black dingy door of the hall and be knocked backwards by the smoke. The only lights in the place were the ones over the tables, so you could easily go missing if you were the size of nothing as I was. 'Is our Sandy in there?' my sister would say—I was christened Alexander like our Dad—No, said the other players: never seen him. I'd be behind the door.

(Mrs Elizabeth Higgins, Alex's Mum: I didn't mind our Sandy being in there really. I thought he was better in there than in mischief, and at least I knew where he was. Besides, he always told me one day he'd be good at something, something with his hands.)

Perhaps Mum thought I was going to be a burglar! In those days, although there was a lot of billiard hall gambling, the game at the top had passed from its 'mis-spent youth' image to an 'older man' image. By then professional snooker had become so conservative and toffee-nosed, and the sport's elder statesmen had it so tied up amongst themselves, that young lads my age would never normally have dreamed of becoming champions. You tended to think of snooker as an old man's game, whereas in actual fact it's a young man's game, as the last three or four years have shown. I think they had it easy, the Joe Davis generation, because it was a closed shop then. Nobody was allowed in. Now, of course, there's just the opposite problem. They're letting people play who haven't a quarter of the ability I had when I broke into the game. When *I* was 22, the likes of Kirk Stevens couldn't have wiped my boots.

I think I know why I became so fast on the shot. At least, you can put this in the Higgins mythology. We used to play a game in the Jampot called Life Pool. Each player had three lives and you used the coloured balls, as I remember, red onto the white, yellow onto the red, green onto the yellow, brown onto the green, blue onto the brown, pink onto the blue, black onto the pink and the white ball on the black. The game was quite dangerous, because there was this big guy who played it called Jim Taylor. He had a sort of growth on the back of his hand, and he was about nine feet tall. He was also what you might call a bad loser. I might be up the other end of the table at full

stretch, pulling off some impossible shot, and out of the corner of my eye, I'd see him coming, with his cue up in the air ready to belt me over the head with it. 'You lucky little b----!' he'd say, not a bit appreciative, so before the balls stopped rolling I'd be round the table. Otherwise he'd have had all three lives off me at the one time.

Of course, as I was competing against men, I was the smallest player in there. At the start I couldn't reach up to the table or hold a cue properly: I was just like any other little kid. But if you play something long enough you become half decent at it. I happened to have a talent for snooker that needed bringing out, and the only way to bring it out was to play, six, seven, maybe eight hours a day. Being small was no great hardship really. I preferred to play men and be at a slight disadvantage, to playing other boys. That would have bored the backside off me. Rumours that I used to have to stand on a box to reach the table are unfounded, and I never climbed on the tables either. Well, not the better tables.

Oddly enough, the players I learned most from in those formative days weren't snooker players—I never had too much contact with them, to be honest. I

Jean and Sandy. Me in charge again, as train driver.

Sister Jean, aged 13, with my first Amateur Northern Ireland Cup in 1968.

out of work myself.)

(Jacky Shannon, later Alex's YMCA team-mate: I used to get the equivalent of 25p pocket money—a lot in those days. I remember one occasion, when Alex was skint as per usual, and I lent it to him to play on one of the big tables. We agreed to split the winnings. He turned the 25p into £6.)

My Dad Alex used to play a bit in the Canine Club, but I never liked it much in there. I preferred the Shaftsbury hall, in Shaftsbury square—a veritable hotbed of snooker. Maurice Gill, the Irish Amateur champion, played there a lot, but he wouldn't have known much about me because at the time I couldn't really play well. I was only a kid, marking for everybody. He was a methodical, steady player, was Maurice.

(Maurice Gill, three times Northern Ireland champion, twice All-Ireland champion: Alex left the Jampot and moved on to the Shaftsbury to meet a better class of competition. He was beginning to improve and he realized it. It got so that the fellows wouldn't play him and he was having to handicap himself. I'd like to think he learned from my mistakes, since he went on to better things. He had an audience, even then, and he'd get very cross with himself if he

Aunt Jean, myself and Jean, my sister.

absorbed most from billiards players, people like Billy Bennett and Sammy Bailey. I never had any formal instruction. I never learned by words, but by watching. The Jampot had about 18 tables, of which I remember 1, 8 and 9 were the best, and hives of activity. It was like divisional football: you gradually gained promotion towards the top tables, to play the likes of Willie Maxwell, Alan Sproule and Georgie 'The Bug' McClatchey.

(Willie Maxwell: Higgy started out marking the results up to earn his stake money to play what we call Sticks. For a 'stick' you'd to have an odd number of players, and it was every man for himself, highest points the winner. And Higgy might mark until he was £1 up, so he could get more games, and this was heavy gambling when we were young. I was sneaking

missed a pot. 'How did I miss this! How did I miss that!' Just like now, on television. Oh yes, he always bobbed his head up. I told him about that.)

I wanted to get away from Belfast when I left school. The Troubles were just beginning to break out when I was 15: before that I remember you could go anywhere and do anything in Belfast, but it wasn't exactly Paradise even then. Very high unemployment, very few opportunities. And I wanted to be somebody. Alexander the Great if possible. So when the time came for me to leave school, there I was, with a new overcoat and a package containing a few bits and pieces and socks with no holes in, saying goodbye to the family home. I was off to be a jockey.

School line-up. That's me with the punk hair, front row, first on the left.
Mum, Elizabeth Higgins.

OTHER PLAYERS TALKING
EDDIE CHARLTON

Over the years we have played a lot of matches—at least 30-odd. Alex is a very nervy type of player that when he's at the table appears to play on his nerves—and it's only at the table, because he's quite relaxed when he's away from it—but that is the reason he plays so quick. I don't think he could look at the balls and concentrate and go slow as some of us do, because it would drive him mad. It's just a quick impulse. Yes I think it *does* bother him to have somebody slow the tempo down. In big matches with Alex, I've always brought the safety into it. But it's a funny game; it depends how you go about it. I attack the balls as much as anybody in the game, but there's got to be a *time* to attack them. Even when Alex is on the defensive, he attacks. Still, there's no doubt about it—he's an amazing player. Nobody else plays the game as he does.

He does take more risks than other people—mind you, that's only when he's ahead mainly. When he's under the hammer like he's been in so many matches against me, he plays it tough, because he's in trouble. He had a prolonged bad run against me when I beat him in the semi-final of the 1973 World Championship: all the marvellous play that he can come up with didn't surface because I kept him under the hammer. But when he's buzzing, when things are going for him and he gets out in front, well, he just plays shots that nobody else would play. He's a *marvellous* potter. It's only the fact that he can't contain himself at times that prevents him from being a really solid, consistent player. To me, a great player has to be consistent, and I've seen Alex playing unbeatable snooker at two in the afternoon and in the evening session he's been like a different player. But that's by the by: he can pot balls from anywhere as well as anybody, and he's a good long potter. As for bobbing his head up, well it's in his timing, and I've seen him play so well doing that, that I'd have to say he struck the ball before he

moved. It's not only his head that comes up—a lot of his body moves. But he's not a big man, Alex, and for him to get the power into some of his shots he's really got to take a swipe at it, and that's exactly what he does.

Over the years that I've watched him and played against him, I've seen him pot some marvellous balls. I've seen him pot ridiculously difficult pots with a ton of running side or check side on the white ball: half the time I'm inclined to think that it's a fluke, the shot's been so outrageous. But he's a good positional player as well, because nine times out of ten when he pots a good ball he's *in*. And he's reasonably reliable when he *gets* in, and his safety play is strong. So adding all that up with the fact that he's a good long potter, good when he gets in close and fairly reliable when the balls are on—that's why he's never far off the top. He's one of the absolute top players, and you know, if he just steadied down a bit and tried to be more consistent, he'd take some budging off the top.

Eddie Charlton with David Vine.

OTHER PLAYERS TALKING
FRED DAVIS

His game is the same as when he won the World Championship in 1972. He's still got that tremendous talent. The only thing that's changed since then is that the effect of his coming into the game, the initial impact, is gone. So opponents are more accustomed to his play and this tends to make it more difficult for Alex. After all, even *he* couldn't continue on the same high level as he started. When he first came into snooker he played without any thought for what his opponent could do, so he played more relaxed—if you could ever use that word of Alex. And if he's not quite so fluent as in '72, not quite so consistently good, it's only because other players have become inured to him. Yes, to a certain degree he's lost his confidence, and his concentration is slightly impaired. He's still capable of playing at the highest level, and although

he's unorthodox, bobbing his head up and so on, he doesn't make the errors that one might assume because he does stay still on the shot—otherwise he couldn't possibly play to the standard he does. There *are* occasions when he does the wrong thing, just like all of us. This is where confidence comes in. All the good things go together in this game, and so do all the bad things. If you've got everything together, everything works out properly for you and the run of the balls goes in your favour. Basically, luck is playing with confidence. Alex has one of the sharpest brains in the game. The only trouble is, because he's better, it's not enough for him just to pot the ball: he's got to do it differently from anyone else. He feels compelled to show off. That's why he sometimes comes unstuck!
Fred Davis.

STABLES
to TABLES

On 'Come on Sparkle' at Epsom.

I DECIDED to become a jockey because I had all the necessary qualifications: I'd always been keen on horses, and I weighed 7 stone. I got a telephone number from somebody and went along to Eddie Reavey's stables near Wantage in Berkshire, for a sort of trial. Not that I dreamed of winning the Grand National or anything like that, as I'd no horsey background. But there are two ways to upset me, even now. One is to insult Muhammad Ali and the other is to criticise Lester Piggott. I've never missed an opportunity of watching them in action, to see their adrenalin flow and how they're the masters of it. They are supreme. They have the knowledge. In horse racing you might only feel that adrenalin for a few minutes; in snooker it can be steadily pumping through your whole body for three hours. But whatever the sport, it's like high octane fuel. It's a drug. You feel super big, and once you've had that feeling, you get it where you can. I suppose, at 15, I thought I might get it from flat racing.

As it turned out, I never had a public ride. The most exhilarating thing that happened to me all the time I was at the stables was that I got into a few fights. They were the same size as me, these lads, and I thumped a couple of them that deserved it. There's a hierarchy in stables from the apprentice jockey down to the stable boy. I was the stable boy. I shovelled the crap. Well, the assistant head lad was seven or eight years older and any time Reavey thought he had a good horse on his hands, this assistant head lad would be the one to look after it. It must have turned his head, because he used to order the rest of us about something shocking. One night it was pouring with rain, and I'd had just about enough of this Little Hitler malarky, so I decided to put him straight on a few points. I set about him in the courtyard. They had to pull me off. This was the first outbreak of an allergy I have, to being ordered about.

Reavey didn't know what went on, really, or if he did he turned a blind eye to it. On another occasion— it was 9 o'clock at night in the middle of winter, and pitch dark—I was riding a bicycle with no brakes, heading back from the shops, when suddenly what should appear on the hill 50 yards from the stables, crossing the road, but the local bobby. Smack, I hit him. I came off the bike, and he was on the deck, so I ran round the back of a barn and took the long way home. They traced the bike back to the stables, but to this day they don't know who was riding it. All they know is, it wasn't Lester Piggott.

I remember some of the jockeys at the stables. There was Willie Currie who alas no longer rides: he rode second in the £10,000 News of the World Handicap 15 years ago and that was a big, big race. The kid just didn't have the strength to ride the horse out. I remember Pat Reavey too: a tragedy that he never fulfilled his destiny. He'd be about 26 now.

So much depends on the rides you get, because a terrible jockey can win on a good horse. I have a jockey friend in Ireland who was a champion apprentice but he's still breaking his heart trying to get rides. You've got to be something really special, and even then for the first six years you're crucified with training and weight problems. I don't think I could have stood breakfasting on a cigar like Piggott, or having two boiled eggs for Christmas dinner. Or taking pee pills and what have you like a lot of them do. I put on weight. After starving myself to death in Belfast, here I was having breakfast at 8.30, dinner at one, tea at six, and getting a lot of fresh air. My weight soared from 7 stone or 7.7 to 9.10 and 10 stone. So I was out. Besides, Eddie Reavey didn't think much of my stable boy abilities. Not to mince matters, he said I was useless. That I was a lazy bum. He was a fair judge, because although I liked the riding, I didn't rate the chores and the mucking out: I used to be a shirker. Still, I was choked when Reavey died recently. I didn't know what to put on the wreath. He was 60-odd, and cancer got him, but when I knew him he was a great trainer, somebody who all but had the National sewn up if the horse hadn't had a mind of its own. It's a hard world.

After leaving the stables I headed for London. I didn't have any clear idea what I'd do when I got there, but I knew this much: I was going from stables back to tables. I still had snooker on the brain. Sometimes I'd wake up in the night shouting 'Where's my cue!'

(Ronnie Harper, snooker correspondent, *Belfast Telegraph*: Alex is remarkable you know. If Alex went to a psychiatrist, the psychiatrist would have to see a psychiatrist.)

To finance my snooker, I got a job in a paper-mill. I just played and practised, working nights for a while. Once I'd finished my shift, it was home for about five hours' sleep, up at one in the afternoon, play snooker until eight or nine at night, have a drink, go back home and watch television, then work from two till ten in the morning, or twelve till eight. There was a lot of self-discipline involved in that routine because I was practising five or six hours a day, every day, and I was tired. People have different views on the necessity of practice in snooker. Some players stay loose naturally, just playing their matches and exhibitions. My body tightens up, so I've got to keep moving all the time. Playing snooker constantly you find your movements can become restricted, and then for no apparent reason, suddenly the cue starts to flow. Generally speaking, I've had to play a lot, and practise a lot, to get that degree of fluidity. I don't believe you can lay off for six months at this game and expect to maintain your form any more than an athlete or a boxer. Or Björn Borg for that matter. He knocks up for two or three hours before a big match to keep his shots grooved. And apart from practice keeping your cue-action loose, it has a psychological effect as well. If you've done the work, you have the confidence. You deserve to be good.

As you get older, you need more work, and although I've managed to stay in the top three or four in the world for eight years, I feel I've done it with my talent alone. I haven't practised regularly for at least seven of those eight years: not a decent four-hour day. I can't, because of trains and boats and planes. My schedule won't let me. By the time I've travelled all day and played all night, and crawled into bed in the small hours, I want to sleep late in the mornings. I know I've burnt the candle at both ends in the past, but my health can get wrecked just like anybody else's, and I've learned the value of sleep. I'll tell you what, though. In my new house I'm having a snooker table installed, so I shall be able to practise when I like. When I've done that, and got myself a cue that can stand the pace, beware Alex Higgins.

At times I got really depressed and homesick on my own in London. I was living around Leytonstone in the East End and after I'd left the paper-mill I'd be playing in Windmill Street till the dawn chorus. I used to catch the N98 from Leytonstone to London Bridge, stopping to pick up all the night passengers— weirdos on buses. I might have fifteen bob in my pocket, going to play snooker, or coming away from playing snooker. The bee's knees in London at that time was a player called Derek Cox, a man of about 36. He was actually a musician, a pianist with the London Philharmonic or the like, but he was widely respected at snooker and I'd play him 15, 20, maybe 25 frames, to the death. This went on for some time but eventually came to a crunch one night, when I'd made six centuries or five on the trot

on a difficult table or something, and this Cox looked at me in a meaningful way. For a minute I thought he was going to say, 'Don't shoot me, I'm only the piano player,' but all he said was, 'Take this, I've had enough.' And then he gave me his cue. After that I presume he went back to Mozart as I never heard what became of him. But that compliment meant a lot to me at the time because in those days, nobody much was paying me any. I had nothing going for me except my own belief in my ability.

It was during this brief interlude of being down-and-out in Leytonstone and Windmill Street that I came across this old guy who played around the West End for money—a postcard-dealer, I believe he was, from Harringay. He used to give me 7 points. He was an inveterate loser: if Muhammad Ali walked in the door he'd have challenged him to a fight. If you beat him and he'd given you 7 points, he'd give you 14 the next game, because he really wanted to lose. What can you do? I took £15 off him regularly for months. I needed the money.

I also met, in those Soho days, Sheila and Tony O'Beirne. Tony was a snooker fanatic and Sheila was a lady. I never forget people who have helped me and they helped me tremendously, those two, encouraging me when I was fed up and broke, and coming all the way up from Guildford to give me £50 for an air ticket to Belfast so I could go home for a couple of weeks, and £50 was a lot of money in those days. They hardly knew who I was, but maybe they knew who I was going to be.

OTHER PLAYERS TALKING
STEVE DAVIS

When Alex is playing at his *best*, he's the best player in the world, but fortunately for the rest of us he doesn't always play at his best because he's got too many bad habits. Technically, I should think Alex and I are just about opposites. Perhaps Tony Meo would come somewhere in between. There *are* things that Alex does right technically but he does lift his head up. When he's on his game he doesn't do it until after he's played the shot, but when he's not, he does it before. It's also true that he plays to the crowd. If they respond to him it makes him feel like God and play accordingly: he goes on one of his purple patches. It can go over the top sometimes: he can lose like that as well. His safety game, when he plays it, is extremely good. He knows the angles and he's a clever safety player, but he's also a bit impatient, a bit of a gambler—the sort of person who likes to get things over with quickly and see the issue settled one way or the other.

It all depends what frame of mind Alex is in. It's the same for the rest of us, but perhaps more so for Alex. I think the more erratic you are, the more difficult it is for you to win over a lot of frames: that's why it's hard for an erratic player to do well consistently in the World Championship. But Alex *can* be very good under pressure. Like in the last frame of his first round match with Tony Meo in the 1980 Championship. If Alex had lost that match, it would have been the third year he'd been in trouble in the first round—he'd had tight matches against Mountjoy, and Fagan the previous two years and lost both of those. That frame against Tony was the best I've ever seen him play under pressure, because his reputation as a match-player was at stake, and it always *is* harder when you're expected to win.

As a potter I think it's pretty obvious to most people that Alex goes for a lot of shots that are flamboyant and he gets a percentage of them that are fantastic. Those are the ones people remember, though there are better potters—Cliff Wilson, for example. Positionally Alex is very good, though he has a slightly different brand of positional play to other players. He's unorthodox. Obviously there are different ways of approaching the same positional shot, and Alex plays them the way he feels. Everything depends on his state of mind at the time. I think you'd have to say that's his major fault. Temperament—I suppose you'd call it that.

Steve Davis.

Steve Davis with UK Trophy.

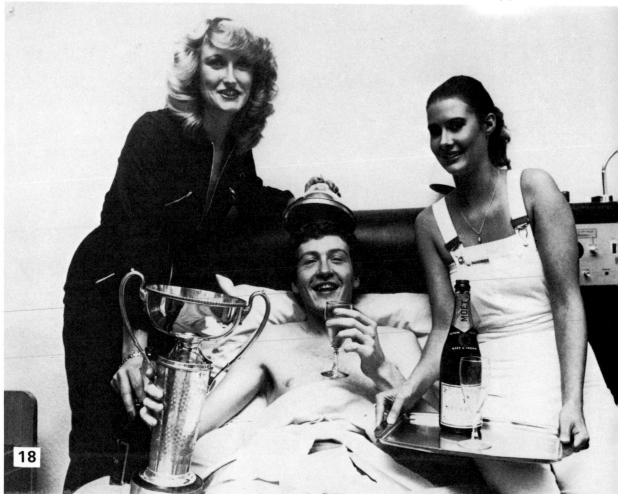

18

OTHER PLAYERS TALKING
PATSY FAGAN

I first played Alex, I think, nine or ten years ago. He hasn't changed. He might have mellowed a bit with age, but his game's the same. He would have to have had a safety game, even in 1972. He would *always* have had a safety game, because he's very knowledgeable about it. Whether or not you use safety depends how the run of the balls goes, but I think Alex can handle opponents' safety play. I don't know why, but I think he likes playing Reardon. He always seems to look confident against him. As a potter Alex is devastating, and he's a great position player. He might get position differently to make it look harder—that's for the crowd, the people in the audience. It makes the shot look more spectacular and yes, it can occasionally cost him matches, though I think that applies to exhibition play rather than important tournaments. Alex does use side with screw where another pro might tend to avoid it. All the pros can produce those shots, but they'd rather not have to. Whereas Alex will deliberately put himself into a position where he *has* to use, say, reverse side with screw. I think it's for the crowd, though a lot of them wouldn't really understand what he's doing. There are always knowledgeable sections of the crowd, but a lot of people who come to watch Alex are just there to see Alex Higgins. Is he lucky? Well, if you take more chances, you're entitled to more luck, and Alex takes chances. I'm trying to cut down, myself.

Alex gets a bit hot under the collar sometimes: he's got a good temperament rather than a great one. But he's a good pressure player.

BACK TO BELFAST

At Mountpottinger YMCA (with treasurer Alfie Sanderson) before my first match in the Northern Ireland Amateur Championships, January 1968.

A FEW months later I was back home in Belfast. I'd no job but I was potting some long reds. This was to be the beginning of my Higgins the Hustler period. I believe the dole in those days amounted to £4.50, so a lot of gambling went on in the billiard halls of Northern Ireland. They say a good boxer has to be hungry: well, some of the billiard and snooker players hustling in the halls of Belfast around then were damn near starving—or they were if they lost.

(Danny Blanchflower, Alex's golfing partner: I grew up in Belfast a little before Alex's time but it was much the same then: there were boys kicking footballs round the streets and a lot of people out of work. Men drifted into the billiard halls who had very little money, and they were playing for all they had. The only light would be the one over the table, and you could see the strain on these characters' faces. It was like a theatre. And I think maybe that's how the game should be promoted today.)

There were four main clubs in Belfast: the Crown in the Shankhill Road, the Oxford in the centre of town, and the two in the Donegall Road I've already told you about, the Jampot and the Shaftsbury. They were clubs where everybody from everywhere used to go and play for money. I came from a Protestant street but I've no prejudices: I'll play on anybody's table. Before the Troubles, Protestants and Catholics could just walk into any billiard club and play what we in Northern Ireland called 'Sticks.' With money so scarce at the time, you might have, say, 12/6, of which a 'stick' would cost you half-a-crown. Losers paid the table, so out of five games you could afford, you had to win one or you were out, marking scores. I was always playing away from home. That's the best way to improve your game, to travel about and meet people in their conditions. There were times when instead of hustling I was the one that was being hustled, but it stood me in good stead because I got better, and I wasn't afraid to challenge a player on his own territory.

The halls were good for me, but I wanted to further my game. I'd no thoughts at first of playing League snooker but if you're ambitious and there's somebody better than you, you naturally go after him. Eventually I realized that, instead of travelling all over Belfast to play, I'd be better off joining the YMCA. It was in ideal proximity to home, and most Belfast and District League players belonged to the YMCA or to constitutional clubs; very few billiard halls at that

21

time played in the Leagues. Actually being accepted by the YMCA spurred my ambitions about League snooker, because I'd been having to mark for about six months for the likes of YMCA players such as Billy Caughey, Campbell Martin and Tom McBride. Officially we weren't allowed to gamble at all. Unofficially you might, and some days you had money and some days you didn't. But they were a good band in there: if I was well off people could borrow from me, and vice versa. It was at this time that I suddenly noticed I had a fan, an old guy, a pensioner, who followed me from the Oxford to the YM, and he used to come in every single day and watch me practising, six or seven hours a day, seven

In play at The Mount in the 1968/9 Irish Amateur Championships.

As reigning all-Ireland Amateur Champion after an exhibition match at Doherty's Social Club, Orchard Street. Presenting the trophy, club president Joe McIntyre; looking on, opponent Donal McVeigh.

A pal of mine, 'Bendy' of YMCA Belfast, with Aunt Jean and my first Northern Ireland Amateur Cup.

days a week. I think his name was Charlie O'Hara and he was a billiards player of real ability.

Once I started playing League snooker, my career took off. People now think maybe I held back for bets in those days when I was hustling, but I was trying *all* the time. I've always been very fair and honest, calling foul shots on myself more than any other player in the game—what credit do I ever get for *that*—and giving myself handicaps. If anything I overstretched myself, because I frequently had to pull out every single ounce of effort to win. At the YMCA I gave the best starts anybody could ever wish for: 80, 90, and even a hundred start. But it paid off in the end. 1968 was a big year for me. I beat Maurice Gill 4–1 in the final of the Northern Ireland amateur championship, and then I beat Dublin's Gerry Hanway for the All-Ireland amateur title, that had previously belonged to Gill.

(Ronnie Harper, *Belfast Telegraph*: The evening before Alex met Gill for the Northern Ireland title match we were in Londonderry where Alex was playing an exhibition. We didn't get home till three or four in the morning, and I told him this was ridiculous, that he'd never be able to play. Alex said Don't worry, it won't affect me. And it didn't: he produced some marvellous snooker the next day. This is typical of Alex. He's a freak of nature. The venue for the final was Mountpottinger YMCA—'the Mount' as it was called—the mecca of snooker and billiards in those days. A front seat was two shillings and the back seats a bob. The place was jam-packed as it always was: in fact the stairs were so congested with people relaying the scores that I had to get to the press room via the fire escape. That's how popular the game was then. Of course, the Troubles did a lot to kill it here. The cross-travel became dangerous, and a cue case could easily be mistaken for a .22 rifle.)

The following year, Bangor's Dessie Anderson took the Northern Ireland amateur title from me at the Mount, but something else happened that was to launch me in the direction of my professional career. In fact, if you want to pinpoint my real start in the game of snooker, this was it. My picture appeared in the *Belfast Telegraph* and *Snooker Scene* magazine, above the caption: 'John Pulman presents Belfast YMCA's outstanding young player Alex Higgins with the Players Number Six UK Team Trophy after their thrilling win in the final at Bolton.' We played Penygraig Labour Club, from Glamorgan, at the

Same trophy, this time with my parents. The lady in the picture is my grandmother, who died at 34.

Bolton Institute of Technology. Billy Caughey of Belfast YM was matched against the Welsh Amateur title-holder Terry Parsons, but things had started rather badly for us.

(Billy Caughey: There were three of them and three of us (Alex, myself and Jacky Shannon), and I have fond memories of it because we were marvellously entertained, presenting some local beauty queen with a shillelah and what have you. The only unpleasant thing about it was, I was on first, and I got what they call 'pulverised' by Welsh Amateur

Champion Terry Parsons. I went down 154 points in the first two frames, so it was up to Alex to salvage the situation as best he could against John Shepherd. Well, our Alex started by making a 56 break, doubling a long red up the table. There was a murmur as the balls rolled but when that red dropped into the pocket there was complete silence. Alex proceeded to compile breaks of 39 and 20 to take the third frame 115–8 in 8 minutes, and the fourth frame 91–27, to put us 17 in front.)

I always knew we could win, because although I was captain I'd elected to play their number two. I put Billy in against their number one because I thought he could hold the bloke and it was just unfortunate that Billy got murdered, but still, I've never been bothered about being behind. The match ended in uproar because YMCA led by only 6 points and it was all on the final black. The black was resting about six inches from the pocket, but the Welshman Mel Jones overcut it and went in-off. It would have been easier to pot it than go in-off. But he contrived to do the latter.

(Billy Caughey: I couldn't see from where I was standing whether it had gone in or not, but I saw Alex fling his arms up in the air and I knew we'd won.)

That match turned out to be important for me. Local promoter Jimmy Worsley and sportswriter Vince Laverty must have thought I was God's gift to snooker or something because they immediately booked me for £30 for a week to play John Spencer at the Bolton Institute of Technology, receiving 14. I won that, so I decided to hang around Bolton for a while and trade on my ability. I lived in Bolton, Blackburn, Accrington, Oswaldtwistle—within that eight-mile radius. It's not true that I turned up in Lancashire one day with a cue and a small suitcase proclaiming, 'I'm a snooker player, I play for money.' That's paper talk, and I get fed up sometimes with the way journalists mythologise my experiences for me. As my Mum puts it, 'It's like reading about a total stranger.' What actually happened was that I used to play three-hand sticks with Dennis Taylor and Jimmy Meadowcroft and I used to give them 21 start. I'd manipulate the two of them. If Jimmy followed me, I would leave him a shot where he could bring the white down the table, and my gamble was that about six or seven times out of ten he'd miss the shot, but he'd also leave Dennis down the table. And of course I knew Dennis—he hasn't changed a bit—he would play safe no matter what, and my idea was that if I could win following Dennis, then with Dennis playing Jimmy very, very tight, Jimmy would make mistakes and let me in. And I could do this 18 games out of 21; that was half-a-crown a go.

I played in the Post Office Club in Blackburn, and the Elite in Accrington. I was living off my wits, and sometimes I was living pretty rough, but my game was improving all the time, and that was the main thing. As a matter of fact, I had a rush of blood and applied for an entry form for the English Amateur Championships, and somewhere in the country now there must be one happy lad by the name of Reed, whom I was supposed to meet in the first round. I decided against it in the end, because the English

Waiting to go to a League match in 1967, with amateurs Sam and Rex Gilliland.

Amateur is a very long, drawn-out affair—it takes the guts of nine months to complete the home tournament and there's an awful lot of travelling involved. For a normal working fellow in those days to afford the fares and expenses, and with no help at all from anybody, was a daunting prospect. So I thought, instead of investing in the Amateur championships, I'd take the big step and try to become a professional. There was a probationary period; I had to prove to the hierarchy that I could earn a living playing snooker: you couldn't just walk into the game. But I decided to take the plunge.

While I was playing at Blackburn's Post Office Club I met up with Jack Leeming, John McLaughlin, a Blackburn bingo tycoon, and Dennis Broderick. I would play Dennis and Jimmy and if they weren't there I'd play on my own for maybe six, seven, eight hours. I'd play until I'd made plenty of centuries— I've made ten in an afternoon in practice—and then I'd go home and have a bite to eat, go to the pub and have *half* of bitter, because all I could think about was making another century, and back down to the Post Office again, for more snooker. I'd play all night until I made another hundred break. It was an obsession. I might go to a disco or something later, but that basically was my routine, day in, day out, until Jack and John McLaughlin saw the potential in me and agreed to manage me for a bit. They installed me in a better flat, got me dressed up slightly and started to advertise for engagements for me at £25 a night. They put me on £35 a week for myself, which wasn't bad money nine or ten years ago. People who have seen me play only recently have no idea how fast I really am, because that will only come back with practice. When I was in Blackburn, you understand,

I was the speed of light. This is why John and Jack decided to call me 'Hurricane' Higgins.

I don't like the term 'apprentice' professional, and 'probationary' professional sounds as if you're on remand or something, but there I was, marking time. Before John and Jack managed me, my sister Isobel wanted me to enter for the World Professional Championship in 1971, and she was willing to give me £100 with which to do it. But although I was playing just as well at the time as I was to do the following year, I don't like to play around with other people's money. So I had to give the World Championship a miss. Maybe it was all for the best, because during that so-called probationary period I played lots of challenge matches, good amateurs and even one or two professionals up and down the country. I was honing my game to match-sharpness. I was getting ready.

At an exhibition game in 1971.

OTHER PLAYERS TALKING
TERRY GRIFFITHS

It's very difficult to speak on his technique because he's so unusual. His positional play is very good, of course, that's why he's so consistent break-building, but he positions differently from all the other players. You can guarantee it that in his breaks, if he puts 20 balls together he'll play 6 or 7 different positional shots from what other players would do, with the same result. I'm not talking about the gallery shots. I'm talking about in a normal break. Alex will play to use extremes of side and screw rather than take the simple way out and play the percentage positional shot. He uses more spin, you see. I've noticed, over the last year at least, that he's been trying very hard to eliminate those simple mistakes that have been the dark side of his game. He's certainly tried to play more defensive than he used to. His safety game is very, very sound, but if he's played six or seven good safety shots and he still hasn't got an easy opening off them, then he'll try a long shot and either pot it or leave his opponent in. His patience tends to run out a shot or two before other players—it's like dangling a carrot in front of a donkey. If you put a ball out down the bottom somewhere and he sees there's a possibility of getting it, he finds it very, very difficult to turn down. It's not true that this is a big advantage to his opponents, because you know with Alex, when he goes for that shot, that there's a 50–50 chance of him getting it. In fact he's more likely to miss an easy shot than he is one of those difficult shots under pressure.

Playing against Alex, the one thing you don't want to do is to smack the pack all over the place and see who pots the most, because he normally comes out on top. Why does he break his tips? Well, I hit the ball hard, but nobody tries to get the amount of spin he does on the ball, with power. Although he's very thin and he looks frail, he's a very, very powerful hitter of the ball you see. I love watching him play. He's so exciting, even when he sits down at the table. Somebody told me yesterday during our match, 'I'm going to have a look in this ashtray to see if he smokes more cigarettes than you.' And I said the difference is I take 50 puffs and he takes three out of every cigarette. I was watching him sitting down there yesterday and honestly, it's comical though. I'm just the same, I suppose, except I don't do it as quick as he

does: he sits down, lights a cigarette, chalks his cue, files his tip and has a quick drink—all in one movement! I watched him playing Fred Davis in the UK Championship, and he missed a ridiculously easy shot in the afternoon session. I said to my wife, sitting next to me, look at that. I'll bet he's going to do something spectacular now. And the next visit he made a 60–odd break out of nowhere, and I thought, oh God. Bloody waste of time trying to work this guy out playing snooker.

Terry Griffiths, Benson and Hedges Masters winner 1980.

Terry and wife Annette and the 1980 Master trophy.

Terry Griffiths, Benson and Hedges Masters winner 1980.

Right: Terry Griffiths, with moustache.

OTHER PLAYERS
PERRIE MANS

Pigeon fancier Perrie Mans with myself at the Benson and Hedges Masters.

THE YEAR OF THE HURRICANE

1972 was my year, my property, my personal piece of calendar. It was the year when everything changed, not only for me, but for snooker, and whatever happens in the future no one can ever take that year away from me. It's in the annals of the game.

It started right, even. On January 7th in Graigna-managh, County Kilkenny, I became Irish Professional Champion, beating Jack Rea for a title he had held for twenty years. The score was 28-12, and although the match was scheduled to finish at the Aberdeen Room, Gresham Hotel, Dublin on January 8th, by then the issue was settled.

(Jack Rea: The match was played over a week, nine frames each night at a series of venues. Alex won 5–4 the first night and that set the pattern until the Friday, in Limerick, when he put a new tip on his cue. That night he Hurricaned me 9–0, and that was what won him the Irish Professional title. At the time, Alex had no safety play at all. He was a pure attacking player, willing to gamble on position. And because he was then, and still is, a very much better positional player than anybody gave him credit for, he could pull if off. That Friday night in Limerick he broke me, really. He had the crowd behind him right from the start. It didn't bother me: I'm a little long in the tooth for that. But he had truly great natural ability.)

I've always had tip problems: I must have found one that night that was half decent. I break them with monotonous regularity because I put so much power into my shots and I use so much side—it's like a blade to control. The point of contact on the ball and the point of contact on the cue tip are only the size of pinpricks. You catch one wrong and it goes through the tip like a knife. The problem is compounded for me by the fact that I use very thin tips: I find thick ones too spongey. You have to break them in, especially for my sort of snooker. At the time of my match with Rea some journalist wrote, 'His uncanny use of the screw shot would make many a pro blush.' Not that they'd seen anything yet.

The build-up to the 1972 World Championship, which in those days was played over a prolonged period rather than condensed in the Wimbledon fortnight style of today, began in 1971. In February the draw was made for the following year, and A. Higgins was placed in one of the qualifying sections. As fate would have it during these pre-championship months, I kept meeting up with John Spencer, the reigning World title-holder. I played him in a series of £200 challenge matches, and I'd played him before I turned professional, receiving 21 start. I remember telling him that I thought I was good enough to turn pro then. He didn't directly try to discourage me— well, he couldn't have done—but he didn't exactly slap me on the back and say welcome to my world either. So I said to myself, Look babe (though I may not have used clichés like that at the time), there's no reason why you're not as good as Spencer. In fact, with experience, you'll be better. Better than John Spencer at his best. That's when I decided to scratch from the Amateur Championship. I thought, well, screw that for a game of soldiers. I'll do the probationary professional bit instead.

I also switched managers. There's nothing acrimonious about it: I invited John McLaughlin to my wedding if it's anybody's business, and we're still friends. But two of the kindest people I've ever met, managers or anything else, have been Dennis Broderick and Jack Leeming. I'll give you an example of the sort of thing Jack used to do for me when I was living in Accrington. I saw this suit in a Bolton store. It wasn't a king's ransom, maybe £35 or £40 (players pay upwards of £200 for a suit nowadays), but I'd set my heart on it, and I hadn't any money. I kept on at Jack for weeks and weeks about it and decided I was getting nowhere. Then suddenly one day he said hop in the car, and drove me to Bolton. I got the suit. But it wasn't just that. Jack would try to be tough with Higgins, as most people do, yet he would weaken slightly for me in small ways. He was a very nice guy.

(Dennis Broderick: His first professional engagement was to play Graham Miles, in Walsall. I went to pick him up at 11am. He wasn't up. I had to drag him out of bed and he got ready going along in the car. We got to the venue and he made a hundred break in 3 mins. 55secs. Sometimes we did wonder what we'd taken on. Well, not sometimes. All the time. His first

Christmas with us was very exciting. He played at Accrington two days before, and we gave him his wages, his Christmas presents and his flight ticket to see his family. About 3 in the morning my phone rang. It was Alex. 'Hello' he said, 'I'm at the Ace of Spades', about three miles from where I live. 'What are you doing there, Alex', I said. 'I'm skint. I've lost it all at roulette. Can you pick me up, I've got to get home'. He still had his flight ticket. No money. Cleared the lot. But he's not a bad lad, really. Everybody's been on to him, and he's his own worst enemy sometimes, but he's a terrific personality in his own way.)

Meanwhile, John Spencer was giving quotes to newspaper writers such as, 'You say he's quick and so he is, but he will be better when he slows down.' I eat that sort of thing for breakfast. I was also making progress through the lower reaches of the Championship draw. I beat Ronnie Gross 16–5 and Maurice Parkin 11–3 in the qualifying competition, and then came Jack Rea in the first round of the competition proper. This was in November 1971 before I'd actually taken his Irish Professional title, but I knew I

Dad with some of my trophies in 1973.

had the beating of him. He broke off and I stepped in and cleared the table with a 133 break. I'm a rhythm player, and once I find my rhythm like that, I'm rolling. I beat him 19–11, for a place in the quarter-finals.

If I ever had a hero as a kid, I guess it was John Pulman, who was World Champion for 12 years. During the years I was growing up, Pulman was invincible: a brilliant potter, a tactician, and foxy in the safety department. Well, who should be standing in my path now but old JP himself. I always used to call him 'Mr Pulman' when I saw him around the circuit. One night he was playing David Taylor in the quarter-finals of the 1970 World Championship at Grimsby Transport club, and seeing me at the bar he said, 'John's the name.' I'll always remember that, though he's insulted me a good bit since then, on and off! In the 1972 quarter-final he was wily as ever, slowing the tempo down, waiting for me to make mistakes, and some people predicted his safety game would eventually draw my horns in. They were wrong. I beat him 31–23. Pulman said of me, 'He's good, very good, and I've no doubt will go far.' I was so excited about beating him I don't think I actually went to bed for a couple of nights.

Next came the semi-finals, and the match that turned out to be the real cruncher for me. My opponent was the reigning World Billiards Champion Rex Williams. I've never understood what motivates billiard players. Can you imagine that— you get dressed up in your lounge suit in the afternoon, you go on, you break off and then you sit there for the rest of the afternoon. You don't get a shot. Then you go back to the hotel and change from your lounge suit into your evening suit, and you go back and still don't get a shot. And the next morning you get up and shave and go back in the hall and the guy's still at the table. That would drive me to distraction. Anyway, I knew I was a better snooker player than Williams, despite the fact that I was the underdog going into the match. I'd no doubts about my ability. I might throw silly games away here and there, but I could feel the momentum building up, that I was on my way to the Big One.

Over 61 frames, though, I was inexperienced. I almost made a fatal mistake: I didn't treat my opponent with enough respect until it was very nearly too late. At one point early on I lost nine games on the trot. Even when I'd lost the eighth consecutive frame I thought I could still stop the rot, I could still do it. So

I stuck to my guns, to my attacking game. When I lost the ninth, though, it was time to regroup. While I was running this guy was evidently going to keep sneaking through. I was going to have to buckle down. It took me three days and five sessions to get back on level terms, but I did it. In fact I went two in front in the last session, 30–28, but he pulled those back. I knew I wouldn't be the one to crack, because though I can't vouch for anybody else's temperament, mine had been forged in the fiery furnace. That gives you a lot of faith. The match stood level at 30–30 and in the decider he took a 20 point lead. Then he did it: he missed the blue that I suspect has haunted him ever since.

(Rex Williams: That blue could have changed the direction of both our careers. I knew I'd lost the match, but it's water under the bridge as far as I'm concerned. You can't do anything about it afterwards. The blue wasn't that easy. I potted a long red and I came up the table and kissed into another red over the middle pocket and finished up just below the middle pocket tight on the cushion—absolutely dead tight. I had to play it slow across the nap to get onto the other red. Now, had I been two inches off the cushion it would have been easy. But as it was, this was one of those shots that under extreme pressure was missable. Anyway Higgins stepped in and took four reds, four colours and laid a real cracking snooker. I can remember it: he screwed one and left me straight behind a ball that was on the bottom cushion, and I was in dead trouble. I couldn't do anything. I lost the match *then*. Higgins has certainly got a good temperament but I still think, had he not played Pulman in the previous round, that he wouldn't have beaten me. He has a very good brain for snooker, and in that long match against Pulman he learned enough about safety to beat me in the semi-final.)

So now I was in the World Championship final. As fate would have it, there was a sort of dress rehearsal, the Park Drive 2000 final, played the very evening before the big match, and played against Spencer. At one point I was leading 3–0 and I lost 4–3. Water off a duck's back. I backed myself to beat Spencer in the World Championship, at 10–1, 4–1, 2s, and later, 6–4 over seven months. And I believe I may have mentioned the fact that I was going to win, so if anybody was backing Spencer on the strength of his performance in the Park Drive, that was their look out.

OTHER PLAYERS TALKING
TONY MEO

He's a very open player. He's not the type that likes to hang about; he likes to go for the shots. Like, a lot of players won't go for a ball unless there's a certainty of getting it, which is a percentage game. But Alex would rather take a chance on getting it and winning the frame. I think that's the best way to play. I agree with that. You've got to take chances. If he makes up his mind to play safety, he's one of the best, and on his day he's a very good positional player. It all depends how your mind is: every player's the same. It depends how you feel on the day. You never wake up the same, do

you. When Alex won in 1972 he didn't know how to play safe then, did he. But now he's developed a safety game, because he had to. You can't go for everything nowadays because there are too many good players about, and you can't get them all, not every day. But he's always fairly confident of himself. I wouldn't say he's got a *great* temperament but he plays well under pressure. Well, he beat me, didn't he, in the 1980 World Championship on the odd frame, though I had my chances. He won 10–9, but he had to win the last two frames—that was good under pressure, because I was the underdog, and he was expected to win. There's more pressure on you if you're expected to win. I beat him in the Canadian Open semi-final, 9–7 when I was 18. He beat me in the Gold Cup. In fact he slaughtered me there, 4–0, and I was playing great. We're fairly even in exhibition play. He's even more open in exhibitions—he goes for nearly everything.

He plays to the crowd most of the time. He can't help it; it's the only way he knows how to play, I think. He breaks his tips because of the sheer power of the shots he plays. And that can alter the outcome of a match, because the tip is the most important part of the cue. Players like Alex and myself use a lot of side and screw: a lot of amateurs would never dream of using it because they're not confident of bringing it off. It's the same with plain ball professionals— players like Eddie Charlton—who haven't been brought up that way: they're playing out of the book. They don't take many chances. I don't think Alex has any preferences as to the type of player he's up against; I don't think it matters who he plays. On his day he isn't worried about it, I don't think. What's going to happen to his game in the future? Well, there are a lot of good new players coming up, obviously, but I don't think Alex will change. Thirty-one. Well, that's not old, is it?

Tony Meo covered in champagne.

OTHER PLAYERS TALKING
DOUG MOUNTJOY

I can quite believe Alex when he says he's made ten centuries in an afternoon practising. I've seen him practise like that: once he was down to nine reds he'd chuck the game in. He was only interested in hundreds. Alex isn't really taking that many risks when he's potting. I take 'risks' myself, but I wouldn't say it's actually taking a risk. He's potting good balls, and he's confident he's going to pot them. He's quite capable of pulling the shot off, so it won't be a risk, not to him. What's he like as a positional player? Well, he's very good in actual fact. When he wants to be. Sometimes Alex will do something, though, just for the crowd. This has got nothing at all to do with position. He might have an easy positional shot on, but he'll do the outrageous. Many times I've seen him with a brown on its spot and he's half-ball to stun onto the side cushion for the blue—and he'll screw it right onto the top cushion with stacks of side to come off the top cushion for the blue, when there was no real necessity. This is Alex: this is what he's

known for, this type of thing. I think his game has changed quite a lot since 1972. He's slowed down an awful lot—he's not as impetuous. He's still fast around the table—that's his nervous energy—but he's a lot slower on the shot and he's a lot more consistent now because of it. You've got to slow down. He's not a safety player by nature, definitely not. But when I won the UK Professional Championship in '78, that's all Alex did, in actual fact. He played safety right from the start to the finish, and David Taylor beat him in the semi-final. David Vine interviewed him afterwards, and he said 'I've never seen you play so much safety, Alex.' He said, 'That's the way the game's going.'

THE BIG MATCH

THE venue for the 1972 World Championship match was the concert hall of Selly Park British Legion in Birmingham, not far from Edgbaston cricket ground. What it lacked in size it made up for in audience participation. It was bedlam in there, with chairs being shoved about, pint pots crashing, and all 500 spectators passing the time of day and strolling round the table while you were lining up your shots. Definitely not for players of the nervous disposition I'm reputed to have, 'living on a razor's edge' and what have you. There was no TV coverage because snooker was in its infancy so far as the media were concerned. As a matter of fact, apart from *Pot Black* in colour, it was the coming of the saviour, i.e. myself, that brought the game to the public notice. Thames TV did a documentary on me shortly afterwards that did very well in the ratings. I have a televisable personality, you see.

Anyhow, here we were in this tumultuous place. I've got a lot of respect for John Spencer: he'd been World Champion twice and he'd beaten me 7 times in our 11 meetings, but I knew he didn't like playing me because he never knew what to do to leave me safe. I terrify him. And in 1972, when I was potting from all points on the compass, I terrified him worse.

The opening day it was nip and tuck. We halved the afternoon and evening sessions. The chief talking point was my so-called 'luck' in missing three snookers and leaving the balls safe each time. I think a lot of players nowadays make use of deliberate misses. The referee doesn't know: I mean, you can miss a ball, with expertise, by a few inches, and it's a hard decision. But when I was getting out of snookers off three or four cushions in this match, I was actually playing to hit the ball. In later sessions, I was to put myself in trouble genuinely trying, and it might occur to another pro in the same situation to play a deliberate miss and get safe. I was playing the game straight, as referee Jim Thorpe confirmed afterwards. A lot of people also commented that I was 'lucky' with the run of the balls. Well, if I'm often lucky, it's only because fortune favours the brave.

(John Spencer: He's lucky! No, I'm only joking. I don't think he has any more luck than the rest of us. In

38

the end, it's only the winner who's lucky anyway.)

(Kirk Stevens: I think you make your own luck at this game.)

(Terry Griffiths: I believe that if you do tend to attack more then you get more of the run of the balls. Besides, Alex gets his fair share of bad luck, the same as everybody else. He does tend to spread the balls all over the place, so he's bound to have runs of good and bad luck, and by that I don't just mean fluking the balls, but leaving the balls in a very open position. Sometimes there's no ball pottable to his opponent; sometimes they all are.)

(Tony Meo: He goes for more ridiculous shots, right? And when he misses everybody thinks he's lucky if he gets out safe. Sometimes he does have the luck, but it can run against him. You tend to notice it more with Alex, because he goes for that many more balls.)

I had a valet while I was staying in Birmingham, a big fat guy called Bernard. I never like getting up early in the mornings anyway and at the time I was going to bed late. Bernard's job was to walk into my room and give me a great big slap. This was the only way to waken me, because I'd been out till 4 in the morning, and then I'd change and go down to breakfast. I don't normally like to eat until 11 or 12, but as I wanted to practise before I played, I'd no alternative. It was the same every morning: I'd be picking at my breakfast and suddenly the plate would disappear. Bernard weighed about 20 stone and he hated to see food wasted. They were nice breakfasts, too, at this guesthouse where we stayed. It was about 150 yards from the venue.

(Alex's managers at the time, Dennis Broderick and Jack Leeming: Alex stayed in some unusual places in those early days. One week he lived at No. 9, No. 11, No. 13, No. 15 and No. 17 Ebony Street, Blackburn, because they were pulling them down and every night when we went back another one had gone since the morning. He lived at five houses in a week. Anyway, when we took him down to Birmingham he stayed at this little boarding house, called 'The Pebbles.' John Spencer was staying at the Strathallan, and Alex was going about telling people he was staying at 'The *Peebles*.' He's a great lad, is Alex. A nice personality. And in that World Championship, he played fabulous. He was brilliant.)

After breakfast we would nip out to the club and

Portrait of the author as a young man.

I'd practise for $2\frac{1}{2}$ hours. I'm not exaggerating: I'd practise right up until the minute before we were announced at the match table, and by that time I'd loosened up. I was ready to kill, so to speak. And it was just as well, because Spencer was razor sharp for this one. The second day he regained the lead, running off three frames. He had the chance to win the next frame on the colours as well, but he missed the green with the long rest. With the green in the pocket jaws I was left snookered, but I negotiated that and took the frame, potting the green with a double kiss. Spencer made a 109 break to lead 9–7 but I pulled back the fifth frame of the day with a snooker on the pink, and levelled at 9–9 with a typical Higgins manoeuvre. I began by attempting a long red but hit the brown first and sent the pack flying. The white ball finished up on the baulk cushion, so Spencer asked me to play again. Never ask me to boil my cabbage twice. I picked off a long red to start a break of 41, finishing with a snooker behind the brown. Spencer replied with 46 to lead 50–49, but I cocked hat doubled the last red for a 22 break. I went on to take the frame 77–50. In the evening session Spencer drew away to 13–11. I fouled a ball with my shirt sleeve and I missed a black from its spot. It was one of those nights.

The third day began badly for me as well. Spencer extended his lead to three frames and though I kept closing the gap, I couldn't quite nail him. Not until the last frame of the day. People still talk about that one. Early on, I was awarded a free ball. Spencer queried it, but the referee stuck firm. I made 15, to lead 41–9. Spencer potted a red, but miscued bridging over some reds to pot the pink. At his next visit he made 17, to trail 27–57. Then came our little spot of bother. I snookered him on the last red, which lay alongside the pink. Spencer played a forcing shot off the bank and the ref called a foul, ruling that the cue ball had hit the pink first. Spencer threw a fit. He said he hit the balls simultaneously. If that were the case, I should have thought it's got to be a foul anyway, but Spencer was up in arms about it and didn't simmer down until 40 minutes after the frame was over. I was awarded a free ball, in any case, and Spencer conceded at 27–71 to leave the match all square at 18–18. Now, if Alex Higgins had caused a furore like that, they'd have probably carried me out feet first, disqualified and cashiered from the ranks, but Spencer had his own way. What happened now, unprecedented in Great Britain or in a World

Championship match, was that we had linesmen brought in to assist the referee for the remaining sessions. I ask you. Looking back, I think Spencer was taking unfair advantage because I was just a kid. But at the time I decided my best course was to keep my lip buttoned. What I lacked in experience I'd make up for in talent. And in the end, my cue would speak for me.

I knew inside that I was wearing Spencer down. He was playing beautiful snooker as well, but I didn't think his concentration was as good as mine and I felt I could absorb the pressure better than he could. The next day—the Thursday—proved me right.

I opened my account by winning the first frame after a safety duel, 60–52. Now I was in the lead, 19–18 in the match. In the next frame there was yet more speculation that I played a deliberate miss, in front of line-judges, referee, the recording angel and Uncle Tom Cobley. The fact that Spencer didn't appeal, I think, speaks for itself: I'd made a genuine attempt to hit the ball on. Spencer took the frame, to square. I won the next two, 75–29 and 75–11. Spencer retaliated, taking the last two frames of the session to leave us even-stevens going into the evening at 21–21.

On the Thursday night, though, I got a good run of the balls, and I took John Spencer to the cleaners. I won six games on the trot. Clive Everton, documenting the match for *Snooker Scene*, wrote, 'Higgins opened up as if he was playing a lighthearted knockabout as pots flew in from every conceivable angle.' Either the balls had recognised their new master, or the fates had turned against Spencer. The following morning, there was a power cut. We'd been plagued by power cuts throughout the proceedings, squinting our eyes up at times to look at the balls by the light of a mobile generator, but this particular cut was the clincher. Spencer got into his hotel lift with his wife and there they were, stuck between floors for twenty-five minutes, while I was making my way from my own bijou hotel, The Peebles, to practise in the British Legion billiards room, knocking up with a break of 111 in under four minutes. Not my best time, but better than being stuck in a lift.

I opened up my performance at the match table with a 50 break, taking the frame 90–15 for a match lead of 28–21. But now I'd driven Spencer's back against the wall, and as invariably happens when you do that to a champion, he came out and hit me with everything in his locker. My lead dwindled from six to four frames. Somebody had written a poem the previous evening about Spencer drowning in Irish stew: perhaps he got to hear about it. The afternoon session I finished 29–25 in front; the evening session it was 32–28. Spencer was playing very high class snooker, and putting me under a lot of pressure.

The sixth and final day I think a lot of the pundits were predicting that I'd had my little fling, that Spencer was about to reel me in. In my pre-match practice I made two century breaks in five frames. I knew I had to keep my cue action smooth and I also knew I had to keep my head. Since the Monday I'd been given the third degree by journalists, broadcasters and television interviewers and it was beginning to get to me. It was hard to sleep and even harder to wake up, and I needed a good belt in the face from Bernard to get me operative on the crucial morning. I took the first frame of the day with a 40 clearance after Spencer missed a long yellow, but then he started to climb all over me. The next frame I don't think I saw the table: he amassed a 123 break to the blue for a 123–0 whitewash. It didn't intimidate me: I knew he was punching himself out producing that form, and that I could do the same at my first opening, but unfortunately he continued in the same vein, 76–21 in the third, 85–42 in the fourth. The match score was now 33–31. If Higgins was going to crack, now was the time.

The balls weren't sitting very well for me, but I got out of my chair, chalked my cue, and took the fifth frame 96–16 and the sixth 88–14. John Pulman was to say afterwards, 'You've got to give the kid credit, because he's hardly had a shot for three frames and then Spencer makes two negligible mistakes and he's snapped up the two frames to go back four in front.' I think that was what broke Spencer in the finish. By the evening session I only needed two frames for the World Championship, and I made no mistake about those. Spencer made 14 and missed a pottable red; he led by 38–28. I cleared up to take the frame 62–38. In the next frame, my last and best, I coasted home on a 94 break, my highest of the match, and a 46, to shut him out 140–0. I was World Champion, by 37–31.

I'd told everyone I was going to win. What I'd planned to do, as a matter of fact, was to shout, 'I'm the greatest!' or something along those lines, as the winning ball went down. But when the time came, I bit my lip. I'd shown them: I didn't need to go raving on about it like an idiot. I didn't need to go raving on about the prizemoney either. £480. These days, they fine me more than that!

OTHER PLAYERS TALKING
JOHN PULMAN

I think what causes him to be different from the majority of the other players is the fact that he's got the quickest brain the game has ever seen. He seems able to assess things so very, very quickly, and this is what makes him play so fast—in addition to his being highly strung anyway. His quick assessment of the game is absolutely fantastic, and allied to that is his tremendous cue ball control: he can do things with the cue ball that few other players can do. Tremendous screw power, and side—he can put more side onto a ball than any of the others. He plays a lot of power shots, of course. He gives them a bit of a bashing. Check side and running side he plays with far more power than most of the other players. So far as

'playing to the galleries' is concerned: people tend to think of Alex as being very adventurous; always having a go. But when the occasion demands he's as good a safety player as anyone in the game. He's got tremendous knowledge of it. All his opponents will tell you that. I don't think his game has changed since he won the World Championship, and as for saying he doesn't practise: well, I'd take that with a pinch of salt, quite honestly. Because he is such a fanatic for the game that I imagine if he went a day without playing, he'd die. It's so much a part and parcel of his life. This is why, when he goes to a one-night exhibition and he doesn't feel he's acquitted himself as well as the public would like, he'll go on playing.

42

Another pro probably wouldn't do that. Of course, it's completely wrong to jump up on the shot as Alex appears to do, because you're supposed to stay absolutely still, but I think if you took a slow motion film of Alex you'd see that he plays the stroke before he moves. Otherwise he would never pot the balls he does.

John Pulman receiving presentation from Ted Lowe.

OTHER PLAYERS TALKING
RAY REARDON

Alex's game is exciting. I like playing against Alex myself. I know what he's going to do: that normally it won't be orthodox, it'll be something different, even though he'll probably finish up in the same place. That's exciting from an opponent's point of view. He always knows, although he doesn't appear to work it out, what he's going to do. It's not all bang, crash, all that business. He knows where the ball's going. He's a very skilful player, and he reads the table quick as a flash. People don't understand Alex's style of game. He's a top class professional and he knows what he's doing when he's putting, say, deep screw with reverse side on the ball, or running side, backside, any sort of side. The only side he hasn't attempted is suicide. But he's so exciting to watch, you see, especially when he's on song— and on those occasions he's practically unstoppable. He's not really taking risks at all. If he misses a shot, you usually find he's put the white in such a position that he hasn't left anything easy on. Good safety player, great defensive player. Lovely touch. Great snooker player, great player for getting snookers. A lot of nervous energy, but then that's his life, isn't it. He leads a very fast life. He's worn out two bodies already. But speed isn't really that important in this game because it doesn't matter how fast the ball goes in the pocket, you still only get one for a red and seven for a black. But Alex could play with a broom handle, he's that type of person. He may say he doesn't think much of his cues but every time he picks one up he knocks a hundred break in with it, so they're all the same to him. Nobody else can do that. He's unique in that respect. Why hasn't he won the World Championship since '72? Well, when I play Alex, he always plays on song. If he treated all his other opponents with the same respect as when he plays me, he would have won the title two or three times. But he doesn't, and as a result he makes mistakes and he loses. It's probably true that he plays to the galleries. The crowds turn him on, you see. If no one supports him in that respect, with the applause and tears, he's not on song. He gets his adrenalin from the audience. They help him. They lift his game for him.

44

TROUBLE

WINNING the World Championship was one thing; defending it was quite another, because between times I lost my cue. My original Burwat champion got broken about four months later, and it can take years to get used to a replacement. Various cues that I had were always patched up and they didn't seem to suit me. In general, I've been messing about with different cues

1973 was a fraught year for me. Here I am practising before my World title defence.

ever since, and I've never found anything that I've got 200 percent confidence in. It's only my ability and talent that have carried me through. I'd always had a safety game, but now I was going to have to use it. If you've no confidence in potting the balls with a strange cue, you've got to play more safety to give yourself a chance to get in at the top of the table. Even now I'm not happy with the cue I've got, though it's just been re-butted and Fred Davis says it's like a piece of steel. I keep harking back to my first and best cue. There are about 40 lying about in my house and I

keep on experimenting, doctoring one up at a time and trying it out. But it's like looking for the proverbial needle in a haystack. My first replacement cue was short, and in those days I wasn't into sophisticated carpentry, inserting pieces of wood and what have you. So I got a couple of nails and some plastic padding and cobbled it together in a makeshift way. It wasn't as good as my old Burwat Champion. I'd lost my cue, and I'd lost my confidence. I was walking wounded. I was easy meat for anybody.

Everything started to come unglued. I've got myself onto an even keel now, but in those early days I spent everything I got. I did what a lot of people do who've had nothing and suddenly find themselves comparatively well off: I blew it. There were a lot of newspaper stories about my activities, womanising,

high-rolling, smoking, spending and carousing. The hell-raising reputation of Hurricane Higgins which to this day precedes me wherever I go was partly my own fault and partly the fault of a very low denomination of press men who followed me about looking for 'incidents'. I don't expect the press to be forever writing, 'Alex is a hell of a nice bloke,' and OK, I'll admit to having the odd bet and that before I met Lynn I went out with all sorts of girls. But I wish press people would confine their imaginations to the quality of the snooker I play, and just give the controversy a rest. There are things I could stick in the newspapers about some of *their* activities, but I don't. Newspapers are supposed to be fair and objective, and if press men are assigned to snooker tournaments and don't understand the game, at least

At Millhouse Lane, Sheffield after a win over John Spencer in 1974.

they should have the brains to know who's pleasing the crowds. Ninety-nine percent of what journalists have written about me over the years has been a load of crap. Even now, most of them still spice up their articles on Higgins with references to his hell-raising days. They can't describe a 146 break in Leicester without straining to mention some court case or misdemeanour of mine.

My managers for a while were West and Nally, and through Patrick Nally in particular I think it was arranged that I should be rigged out by Tom Gilby, a leading fashion designer: you know—colourful this, colourful that, red waistcoats, green waistcoats, white pants, green pants, lurex pants. All co-ordinated, to wear at the table. I think one of my WPBSA fines that year was £100 for wearing a green evening suit. I've always taken trouble over my sartorial elegance, only

to be fined for it by the WPBSA, who think you're supposed to play the game looking like a tailor's dummy. I've been criticised for playing in braces, playing in an open waistcoat, playing in a Fedora hat, playing without a tie. I'm a professional snooker player: I need to have freedom of movement for my game, the same as other sportsmen. What I wear on my back is my business.

Everywhere I went there was trouble. Trouble in Hartlepool: I was reported to the Players Association by the Hartlepool S.A. for refusing to continue an exhibition against John Spencer. After complaining several times about the lighting, and being fouled unfairly in the eighth frame, I conceded and walked out. There were four arc lights in the entire hall and you couldn't see the balls for the shadows everywhere. I came to play snooker, not blind man's buff, and I like to entertain people. This was robbing them of their admission money because you can't play decent snooker in conditions like that. Of course, snooker's come a long way since then, but if the same thing happened tomorrow I'd walk out and demand my guarantee as well. I did offer to turn up and finish that match the following night as a personal favour to the organiser, Alan Braithwaite, but as often happens in these situations I was snubbed.

More trouble in Ilfracombe, where I was frogmarched out of a hall after a fracas which had been deliberately started by a guy in the audience trying to get a rise out of me in front of his mates. Now, I knew he'd come to the match to show off and I shouldn't have let it get to me, but at the time I had very little self-restraint. I've always been highly-strung, and I was being rushed from pillar to post on this hectic schedule—plus the fact that I'd just given up smoking as well. I threw my cue at the guy. OK, it was very immature of me.

Another evening, I was due to play Ray Reardon at City Hall, Sheffield. I had a black eye, because I went into some club or other and I was smacked. Somebody just walked over and punched me—no reason; jealousy, probably. I covered my eye—I couldn't see— and then the kicking started. I was taken to hospital and detained overnight. Now, a lot of people would have cancelled against Reardon, if for no other reason than embarrassment about the black eye, but I said, no, I'm going to play. I had double vision, so I bought a patch and tried to practise in it. I tried for hours. Couldn't hit a ball. So I cut a hole in the patch. Still no good. Even dispensing with the patch altogether, I couldn't make a 40 break. But I did play Reardon the following night, because I said I would. I buried him, black eye, double vision and all. The only shots I couldn't get were fine cuts. I had to put the white in position where everything was straightforward.

After I'd transferred from West and Nally and the organising of Simon Weaver to Maurice Hayes of 'Q' Promotions Limited, there were one or two scheduling mix-ups. On one occasion I was booked to play in the Watney's tournament at Leeds, advertised on posters three months previously, and simultaneously I was booked at a club somewhere down Ilford way. I suppose the idea was that if I got knocked out of the tournament, I could play the exhibition. Either that, or somebody thought I had a split personality. Well, I didn't know anything about the double booking: my policy was always to go to tournaments and try to win them. I had to pay £970, I think, compensation. On another occasion, unbeknown to me, I was booked to play in front of 600 Welshmen sitting drumming their fingers at Llay British Legion Club, Wrexham, while I was taking my mother to the station in Preston. The organisers had to refund everybody's 40p ticket money. I paid compensation for that out of my own pocket, and I appeared later at the venue without charge. That misadventure cost me £565.

Trouble at home; trouble abroad. A tour of India, for instance, that lasted approximately one day. I started my first exhibition at Bombay Gymkhana with a 109 break, and then I was reported to have 'offended members by drinking, stripping off my shirt, and insulting behaviour. The B.A. and C.C. of India,' so the report went, 'put me on the next plane home.' Well, I'll tell you what really happened. I didn't think a lot of India. I'd been told that though I was on expenses only, and though it was a poor country, not to worry and what have you, as I'd be recompensed in presents, especially if I made a century break. Well, I made 109, and what did I get? A little tin jug from some millionaire. I thought, India's not for me. The place was a filthy, fly-ridden, revolting tip. A kid came into my room with water and I gave him a Marks and Spencers shirt or something; from that moment, he was in there every 28 seconds. I had to play snooker in these oven temperatures and the sweat was rolling off me. I'm thin now; I don't need to take off a couple of tons. So I undid my shirt—and there was a furore about that.

They didn't have to put me on any plane home. I went of my own accord.

Australia, on the other hand, is a country I like. I went over to play Eddie Charlton in a challenge match at Merrickville RSL Club in Sydney. It taught me something about Charlton: he's a battler, a hard man to beat. I maybe didn't have the respect for him that I should have had, because if I won a session I'd go to the races instead of practising, and he beat me in the end.

There are a lot of distractions out there, actually. I have an emigrant sister, Isobel, and if I wasn't staying with her I'd be holed up in some nice Aussie hotel. I was making the rounds with a professional gambler called Peter Wake. We used to go to the 'trots', to city tennis, and the Boulevard Hotel—having a good time. Peter first approached me at the Merrickville club: he said, 'I'll give you a thousand if you win.' Now, you could understand a gambler saying 'I'll give you a thousand if you *lose*'. I thought this bloke must be a lunatic, but Peter was sincere, and he became a second father to me, and best man at my wedding. He was a genius, a mathematician. We were part of a syndicate, doing the computer racing and congregating in the Glasshouse Bar. Real life characters out of Runyon—I'm very fond of Runyon—there was no Harry the Horse, but there was a Freddie the Scientist, Bobby Dunlop the boxer, from the Coogie Bay Hotel, Fred Clapham from New Zealand, Lindsay Turnbull, Michael McCew. Genuine people—funnier than Runyon's, actually. Peter could have been the best bookmaker in Australia, but he didn't want that. All he wanted was to be the best gambler in Australia.

There has been some bad publicity about my trips Down Under. One incident in particular got blown up out of all proportion. All I can say is, my behaviour at and around the snooker table was always good: I play the game well, I win well and I lose well. What I do in my private life is entirely my own affair. One story I might mention, if only as an example of inaccurate reporting. I was supposed to have been thrown out of a Sydney club for insulting veteran professional Norman Squire and calling him an 'old no-hoper.' After I was thrown out, I reportedly sat in the gutter writing an abject apology on toilet paper before being allowed back in, only to start playing naked from the waist up. Well, it wasn't Norman Squire, it was the owner of the club, Joe Taylor, a very respected man. I apologised on a piece of

With an old friend from Belfast YMCA in Perth, 1973. I was there to play Eddie Charlton.

notepaper, not toilet paper, and after that evening, Joe and I became good friends. I get very annoyed with journalists at times. I did other things in Sydney as well, like going to visit a 19-year-old amateur who'd just had his right arm rejoined above the elbow in the Prince of Wales hospital there after an industrial accident. You don't get to hear about the decent things I do.

Back home, I was still racing round the country. Thames TV made a documentary about Alex Higgins, the wandering snooker player—the travelling, the good times, the hardships. It wasn't all glamour, by any means. It showed what you might call the loneliness and the hanging about on dingy little railway stations as well. I was included in the line-up for *Pot Black* on BBC 2, the first of several intermittant appearances on that programme, and I beat Suzi Quatro, the American rock singer, in a $1000 grudge match at Victoria Sporting Club. It

was the best of five frames and I wasn't very chivalrous about it; I cleaned her out in three straight. Then there were my driving lessons. As anyone knows who reads about snooker, I don't drive a car. It's been the bane of my life, because it places me at the mercy of public transport getting to and from venues: the late trains, the milk trains, the non-runners—you name them and I've had them. Well, I did try to learn to drive. My second time at the wheel I was in a Renault with the handbrake down on the right hand side of the steering column. I was edging out and edging out, and I suddenly spotted this big corporation lorry rounding the corner on my blind side. I panicked. Instead of finding the brake I found the gas. Ding! Straight into the side, and £600 worth of damage. The driver was very decent about it, and we proceeded to go for a drink to calm our nerves. There wasn't really anything wrong with our nerves: it was just an excuse to get a drink in the afternoon.

53

OTHER PLAYERS TALKING
JOHN SPENCER

I don't think you can isolate any one aspect of Alex's game. It's flair that makes him different from other people. He's got what I call a very good snooker brain. He *thinks* the game very well. Does he take risks? Well, generally speaking, the person who plays safe is the person who doesn't think he's going to pot the ball, and I don't think Alex ever takes a risk in his own mind: he always thinks, if he goes for a shot, that he's going to pot the ball. It's only ever a risky shot if you miss it! I've always admired Alex's game. He's a very good player—a very dangerous player, the sort that can win from nothing. He's got a good temperament, and above all he's completely natural. His shots are natural, as opposed to by the book. He's very good, too, with the rest, because he's got short legs. The shorter players usually get more practice with the rest, so they become proficient at it. I don't know why it is he breaks a lot of tips: I don't break mine, though I use side, and it does take the extreme edge of the tip when you use side. Alex goes for some outrageous ones. Tell him he wants to spend some money and buy some new tips!

John Spencer, centre.

John Spencer

MORE TROUBLE

I love horses. Here I am with a foal called Hurricane Mark II in the Isle of Man.

PERHAPS, with all the hullabaloo of those years, the publicity, the mad schedule, and especially the losing of my cue, it wasn't surprising that I didn't cover myself with glory in the World Championships. In fact, during the whole period, I was in the wilderness really. I knew I was too pretty to be a has-been and I knew, and said as much at the time, that I'd still be around when the others were all in their wooden boxes. But so far as World titles were concerned, the Hurricane had blown itself out. My record was so near and yet so far: heart-breaking when you consider snooker was now the centre of more press and TV coverage than ever before. It was the start of the green baize craze I'd helped to create, and here I was, in no luck whatsoever.

Before my title defence I'd given up smoking for several months and started smoking again, and I was generally in a mess, a shambles. I arrived at Manchester City Exhibition Halls and what do I find, but my picture plastered all over a cigarette advert in the programme. It was a sore subject, and they'd no right to use my picture like that. I was defending my title and maybe a little bit nervous: I had a lot of things on my mind. I blew my top. Then I arrived 22 minutes late for the evening session of my match with Pat Houlihan. We'd left early but we were stuck in traffic. Also, my white Oxford bags needed pressing, as I'm a fastidious dresser. I was fined £100 by the W.P.B.S.A. for the lateness and the trousers, because I wasn't wearing the regulation black evening suit—I think I gave them the two fingers but I paid it—and I was ticked off by the tournament organiser Bruce Donkin and booed and jeered by the crowd, though I did apologise. Over the years I think people have treated me very shabbily. I think I'm more sinned against than sinning. Still, I soon knocked in a 70 break and in one frame they were back on my side, stomping the place out.

My quarter-final against Fred Davis included a stoppage for rain: the roof leaked onto Fred's glasses and then dripped on the table. I won that 16–14, but in the semi-final Charlton was waiting to snuff me out, 23–9. I didn't underestimate Eddie. I knew he was a hard man from my dealings with him in challenge matches. He was what you might call relentless and my cue was what you might call useless. John Pulman said afterwards, 'I'm glad Higgins lost. He's dragged the game down.' I like John. I bought him a birthday cake one year, you know. I think he

was 147.

1974 will be remembered as the year of the Push Stroke Affair. I was beaten in the World Champion-ship quarter-finals by Fred, then 61 and recovering from his second heart attack. The referee on that occasion was Jim Thorpe. I was to have other quarrels with him, but this was the first and most famous one. I was leading 13–9 at one point in the match, but Fred was easing back with a lot of tight safety to 13–11, when I was suddenly called for a push stroke. I was in the middle of a 32 break and looking at an easy blue. I play thin balls very, very fine, and I can still get side on them and work the white round. I'd got up close to the blue and probably, had I used the rest, I'd have potted the blue anyway and Thorpe wouldn't have thought of fouling me. But I'm good at stretching, so I didn't bother with the rest. The white went exactly where I'd anticipated: I put side on it to carry it between the yellow and brown and came up for the last four or five reds, of which I only needed two or three to clinch the frame. Lo and behold, as the blue dropped into the middle pocket, the referee calls a push stroke and gives Davis 5 points. According to Thorpe, the cue ball was a sixteenth of an inch from the blue, whereas I'd say it was more like $1\frac{1}{2}$ inches. It certainly wasn't a foul shot. Although Fred wouldn't say anything, he stood aside from the table for a long time, it seemed to me, intimating that Thorpe might change his mind. But no matter how vehemently I

Grimsby, 1973 playing barefoot against Charles and Richard Jackson.

57

With Kevin Langby, Aussie jockey in Australia, 1973/4.

58

protested, Jim wouldn't budge. I think it was a case of the man not wanting to swallow his pride in front of a lot of people, because I'm sure the general consensus among the other referees in that hall in Belle Vue Manchester that night, and among the other players I consulted after the match, was that I'd been robbed. To this day it's well known that if I foul a ball I'm the first to admit it. I'd made every effort to calm down and behave myself for this tournament, and be more composed. Now it was all for nothing. I'd been upset again, and the run of the balls changed after that. I led 14–12, but Davis won the last three frames and I was knocked out of the Championship. It's dead and gone now, but I was disappointed, especially since, if memory serves me, both Spencer and Reardon had decisions over-ruled in their favour that year. I shall have *more* to say with regard to referees *later*.

When the list of players invited to compete in the 1975 World Championships in Australia was announced in May of 1974, I wasn't on it. I'm often not included in the invitations for functions held in Australia. As it happened, I paid my own passage and

Auckland, New Zealand, winter 1973. Here I am with former girlfriend Julie and friends Nyree and Les.

With barmaid, Albert Hotel, Liverpool, 1974.

59

At a venue in Birkenhead in 1975 with Graham Miles.

played anyway. I was rebuilding my game around this time. In December 1974 I'd won the Watneys Open tournament at the Northern Snooker Centre in Leeds, beating Rex Williams 13–4, Ray Reardon 13–11 and Fred Davis 17–11 in the final for the £1000 first prize. It did me a lot of good, because it showed I was coming out of the wilderness. Not winning much since my World title, I began to get the feeling everything was going against me. But a real champion always has something up his sleeve. Look at Muhammad Ali: when his speed left him, the man was so talented that he could tap his reserves, using his brain, inventing his rope-a-dope ruse, letting the other fellow punch himself out and what have you. Well, I needed to get myself cueing properly, and it was handy to be able to play a few safety shots and let the other guy make mistakes. When I was relying on super talent to pot the balls, I knew I could get in straight away. But when you're not quite so certain of getting those long pots—with the top six players of today, you make one or two mistakes and it's all over. When I was at my best, nobody had to give me even half a chance, because I'd go for lunatic shots and I'd get nine out of ten of them. Now, with no time to practise and a cue I couldn't trust, I was having to box clever. To win a tournament like that was a different sort of achievement for me.

The 1975 World Championships were held at various venues all over Australia. I reached the semi-finals and frankly, as a venue for a World Championship semi-final, Canberra Working Men's Club was ridiculous. The draw was pretty ridiculous as well, because we had Spencer, Reardon and myself in one half of the draw and promoter Eddie Charlton in the other half, so if he couldn't get to the final you'd have to think there was something a bit wrong somewhere. I beat the Silver Fox, David Taylor 15–2 and in the quarters I beat Rex Williams 19–12. In the semi against Reardon my tips were all against me. They

Accosted by admirers at the Variety Club, Wakefield in 1975.

wouldn't stay on—I must have cracked or chipped about five during the match and though I pulled up to 10–10 from a disastrous start, Reardon finished me 19–14.

Reardon's had cue problems for the past 2½ years, and although people say he was playing better in 1980 than for ages, I don't think he's been anything like the player I remember in those earlier years. He was a fine safety player, a much better safety player than Charlton, but Ray could also make his 70s and 80s. He could win the game in one or two visits. On the whole, my record against Ray has been very good; I've always fancied beating him because I treat him with some respect and therefore I play a lot of safety against him. I get pleasure out of playing someone generally regarded as a great safety man, because if I can tie *him* up in knots and beat the guy reputed to be the great tactician, it means something. It means Higgins is the best all-round player. In 1975, it wasn't to be: Reardon won his third World title, beating Charlton 31–30. But I was in training. I was working on the 'rope-a-dope' aspect of my game.

OTHER PLAYERS TALKING
KIRK STEVENS

Some people have said, 'When Alex gets beat, then Alex threw it away.' Now, that's not true, because Alex is not the sort of player who'd want to throw anything away. I mean, he wouldn't even want to lose the flip of the coin with you, much less a snooker match. It's just that the game is at a level now where you can't bet your house on who's going to win a tournament: there are too many good players around these days who are capable of winning it. Alex always figures in winning. I think Alex realizes now, though maybe he's been a little stubborn on this over the years, that you need a safety game. Once, he figured he could just pulverize his opponents by smashing balls in from everywhere. *I* like that kind of game: I think it's exciting and I like to play that way myself. But Alex knows now that that's not a game that would last through an entire tournament to win. You have to have the equal amount of respect. Because if you leave men with balls at this level, they're going to hurt you. You make one mistake, and it's not often you get another chance.

Maybe, from the point of view of another player, Alex's positional play is almost as devastating as his potting. But I think it's true that he takes more risks. No two players are alike in the way they approach the game, but if you take, say, an on-form Alex and an on-form Cliff Thorburn, Alex will give you a few more chances than Cliff would. That's the one thing that's different. Not that it would bother Alex to have somebody trying to slow the tempo down: if I was Alex, it wouldn't bother me. Alex wants the game to go his way, which is a good way to have it—you try to impose your style of game on your opponent, rather than have him do the opposite.

I don't agree with Alex that it's a young man's game now: there are a lot of younger players, as much as five years younger than I am. I think it's sort of spiced the roast up a bit, but we all keep learning from the 'veterans' around here. I sit out in the crowd and watch matches and most nights I'll pick up a couple of shots that I've never seen before. I sit there dumbfounded—I'm just in awe. I think, how did he do that? These fellows that have been in the game for years, they've been under the pressures of survival,

really, at the table, and their minds are at a level ahead of the younger players—I think they always will be. The pressure has its effects on people: their hair falls out, or they smoke or drink a lot. But the pressure is what you're playing for. If you went out there and there were no nerves, it would be nothing. The pressure makes snooker: the people, the state of the game, the butterflies you feel inside. It's fantastic. You do it under pressure, and you're a king. You wake up in the morning and you look in the mirror and nothing bothers you. I mean, you feel *great*.

OTHER PLAYERS TALKING
DAVID TAYLOR

I think his temperament is tremendous, personally. The proof of the pudding is in the eating, and Alex has been at the top since before 1972—you can't do that with a bad temperament. I was the first player from England to see him in action, because when I won the World Amateur Championship in '68 I went over to Belfast and there he was. I couldn't believe it, actually. For pure natural ability, he was devastating. He didn't have much of a safety game then: you could tie him in a knot. Even now, though, the point about Alex is that if he feels his opponent can't possibly beat him, he doesn't bother with safety anyway—he's not interested. He just pots him off the table. Nowadays of course you've got to have a safety game. Once these guys like Steve Davis and Terry Griffiths get in, they don't make many mistakes. But I wonder sometimes if it has taken something away from Alex's game to have to play safe. It's a pity really, because he's got this tremendous talent, and he can't show it. If you play safe for ten minutes, when an opening comes along you're not always in a good frame of mind to take advantage of it. You've been 'dull' for ten minutes, and it inhibits you. Considering Alex is such a fast, instinctive player, he copes surprisingly well with percentage and safety players. Positionally he's fabulous. In fact, he can get a bit too advanced for his own good. It gets to the stage sometimes when other players don't know what he's doing. Sometimes, his brain is moving so fast, he overlooks a simpler way that might have been better. But if he doesn't win the World Championship again in the next five years, I shall be very surprised. I think the guy's got great talent.

RAY Reardon loomed large in 1976 as well: he was the man to beat. Most of my press coverage that year centred around my private life—in fact, there was hardly any privacy about it. I was where newsmen like me to be: under public scrutiny. At the table, I don't think my behaviour was ever less than exemplary. I play snooker in a proper sportsmanlike fashion.

Early in the year I made a rather unusual 146 break, the first clearance of its kind ever recorded. It was at Leicester YMCA, where Willie Thorne was making his debut in his home town on one of his 'home' tables. I played Willie the best of 19 and I won 10–nothing: I think I made three or four centuries that night, including the 146 clearance. When I broke the balls, I came down the table and snookered him behind the green. He tried to swerve round but hit one of the colours, sending the white back down the table to finish up behind the green again. I potted the brown in the middle as my free ball, and I potted the green in the left hand side pocket and screwed up the table, opening the pack. I was playing at speed, but they were a very knowledgeable crowd and they knew there was an unusual maximum on. When there were about six reds left, I could have been taking two or three blacks to make 148 or 149, but the balls were all compact around the pink: it had to be a red in the middle pocket and a pink in the bottom, or a red in the bottom and a pink in the middle. A lot of the time I *could* have run through and still been on the black. I didn't, because I was cruising; it was a fast rhythm break. It comprised 16 reds, 10 blacks, 5 pinks, 1 green and all the colours. Poor Willie. I told him he'd have to play for a sidestake the following night and he lost seven frames on the trot and £50.

For the Embassy World Championships there was a split venue. The top half of the draw played at Middlesbrough Town Hall—that was Reardon's half. My half of the draw played at the Wythenshawe Forum in Manchester, the venue for the eventual final. On the face of it, I had an advantage over Reardon, didn't I? Well, what actually happened was that Reardon, who'd won the Benson and Hedges Masters and wasn't bothered about anything whatsoever, had a nice work-out up in Middlesbrough against opponents playing like idiots, whilst I was on a wheel of fire in Manchester, coming through against Cliff Thorburn 15–14 after staring defeat in the face at 12–14 down, and surviving close shaves against Spencer 15–14, and Eddie Charlton in the semi 20–18.

(John Virgo: I was watching those matches. By the

John Spencer and myself with friends in Guernsey. Not a split cue in the place.

time Alex reached the final I knew there was no way he would beat Reardon. He looked played out. Exhausted.)

Reardon warmed up for the final beating John Dunning, 15–7, Dennis Taylor, 15–2 and Perrie Mans, 20–10. I was on my knees. And of course, immediately Reardon gets to Manchester, what does he do but start kicking up about the table. The lights weren't right, the tables weren't right, everything was wrong. I was a bit silly at the time, a bit too easy-going. I had every right to say, 'Look. You may be the world champion, but I'm playing you for your title now. This is the table we've elected to play on and I don't want this table *touched*.' If I'd stuck to my guns, they couldn't have touched it. But like a fool I let him have his own way. Like a silly little boy. These days I'm not quite so easily persuaded.

I was leading 4–2 at the first interval. Ray won six of the evening frames to take the lead 8–5, but on the second afternoon I went ahead again 10–9. This was when Reardon started sounding off about the running of the table, and during the interval they went to work on it, evidently to Ray's delight because he won the evening session 6–1, to lead 15–11. I won the first two frames the following day but the next frame was the turning point. I made a 61 break and I needed another red and another black—but I missed an easy ball attempting the shot left-handed. Reardon made a 68 break to win that game and the tide had turned. He won the match 27–16, to take the £6000 winner's cheque—which shows you how up-market snooker had become since 1972. There was a free ball decision in that final that upset me too. When you feel you've been unfairly treated, it can affect your game, especially playing the sort of snooker I do. The run of the balls changes.

To be right on song for any given two weeks in a whole year is very hard. I thought I was a certainty for the 1977 World Championships. I felt good, I was playing more convincingly than for a long time, I was seeded 2, and as the rest of the year was to prove, I'd turned the corner: I was back in the title business. But I lost in the first round of the World Championships to Doug Mountjoy, 13-12. It was at the Crucible Theatre in Sheffield, and the referee threatened to clear the hall at one point because of the pandemonium that erupted during the final frame.

What happened was, I should have made sure of the pink into the middle pocket, but I was thinking of position and it was just as easy to play for a red as well.

The pink rolled off slightly, and caught the lip so gently that it skimmed round the rim of the pocket and stayed out on the other side. Dougie needed every ball on the table for victory, and he went in and cleared up to the final black. So now it was me. I was just getting down to pot it, making absolutely sure, when somebody in the audience—a policeman as we found out later—shouted that the scores were wrong. It was a black ball fight anyway so it didn't make any difference about one or two points. But I was about to hit the ball. The atmosphere was so charged with tension that I stood up to compose myself, and when I got down the second time, I was flustered. Instead of playing the shot I'd planned before I was interrupted, I just had a whack at it. I missed. I thought I'd got safe, over a middle pocket. It *looked* very safe, but of course Dougie had his now-famous swipe at it along the side cushion. (Doug Mountjoy : I had two choices. It would have been difficult to play safe anyway, but I could have played a safety shot. Or else I could send it down the rail, in which case it could rattle and stay out, or it could go down.) I didn't think he was going to pot it. I don't think *he* thought he was going to pot it; he just didn't know of anything else to do. Anyway, in it went. Goodbye Alex Higgins.

I wouldn't have entered the Pontins Open that year, but for my girl Lynn, now the Mrs. I was disgusted with my luck, because my game had come on in leaps and bounds and I'd nearly got to the stage where I was playing unbeatable snooker again, only to get knocked out in the very first round of the World Championships. Lynn, though, being a bit shrewd, said 'Why not enter the Pontins as a non-invited professional?' I wasn't invited to the Pontins, you see, because I wasn't included in the BBC-2 *Pot Black* line-up at the time. You don't understand the connection? Neither does anybody else. The only known link between the two competitions is Whispering Ted Lowe, a Pontins consultant and *Pot Black* commentator. I was uninvited to both functions. So if Cinders was going to the ball, Cinders had to come through the qualifying competition, just like the rank and file. Well, there were only 864 of us, so it had to be a doddle.

A. Higgins was in Group 14, matches being decided on the aggregate score of two frames. In only my second match I trailed Billy Kelly, an Irish amateur from Manchester, by 104 with just four reds remaining in the first frame. In the second, Billy saw the winning post and he started to get nervous. He missed an easy ball to let me in for a 30 break, and I just kept whittling away at the deficit. I finished up potting a gorgeous brown, and I won that frame on the black to give me a winning 133–121 aggregate. I had a couple of other scares against amateurs— Murdo McLeod, a Scot, took me to the deciding frame, and so did Doug French. But once I got downstairs to play the pros on decent tables, I was snorting fire. I paralysed Reardon 4–0 in the quarters, and buried Fred Davis in the semi 4–0. It was the venom in me: I was deadly. And of course, in the final I played a shy little boy called Griffiths, giving him 21 start because he was an amateur. It was the best of 13, and he led at one point, 2–0. I wasn't having that. I dropped him 7–5. At the prizegiving, I could have made some smart remark about not having been invited and so on, but I bit my lip. The audience said it for me. They were calling out, 'What about *Pot Black*, then?'

After that, I was included in *Pot Black* again. The programme's been an on-and-off affair with me, because of my well-publicised threats to walk out half way through the series and other little misunder-standings. I never really liked playing in *Pot Black* to tell the truth, because, with it being a one-frame competition, it's all very stop-and-start. It's very boring to be hanging about in the studios all day and your life isn't your own while you're recording. I don't think the quality of the snooker has been good over the years because you're hurried too much; you can't relax. They put you in that arena—where until recently you'd nowhere to sit down, you couldn't lean anywhere, and you were totally ill at ease. And the money isn't exactly a king's ransome either. I think I may have omitted to show up for a prizegiving or something like that the following year, so I was excluded from yet another series. But I don't bear any grudges. I'm back in *Pot Black* these days.

Four months after Pontins, I won the $15,000 1977 CNE tournament at the National Exhibition Centre in Toronto. It was held in a large, blue-and-white striped tent. We played in hundred degree tempera-tures, amongst a lot of flies. The flies were looking for a dancing elephant, which was actually in a neigh-bouring circus marquee. There was also non-stop reggae coming from a nearby tent, and a steel band. One day, there was a monsoon-type storm and water ran under the tables. The tables had slate only an inch thick, so the cue ball tended to throw off, and also special pop-out pockets. When it wasn't raining, we

With sisters Jean and Ann at Prestatyn for the Pontins Open in 1977, the year I came through the qualifying competition to win.

played in blinding sunlight, and you couldn't actually see the balls because of the tent stripes in the background. Apart from that, the conditions were absolutely perfect. I like a challenge.

I beat John Dillon 9–1, Cliff Thorburn 9–6 and Reardon in the semi. I led Ray 8–3 but I missed a crucial pink. Reardon won that frame and came back 8–7, but I was playing very carefully. I'd learned my lesson in Sheffield: don't underestimate anyone, do the groundwork first and let your opponent make some mistakes instead of putting your head on the chopping block. I clinched the match 9–7. And I beat John Spencer 17–14 in the final. I was never in any trouble, and special guest at the tournament, Joe Davis, so I'm told, was sitting there shaking his head in amazement at my snooker in that final session. Higgins was back on song.

The year ended as it had begun, I'm afraid, with Mountjoy beating me in the semi-final of the Super Crystalate UK Pro Championships in Blackpool. I was 6–2 down but staging a fight-back and in the midst of a 30 break which was about to amount to something. Suddenly a spectator in the front row, who turned out to be a retired Scottish bookie, called out to Doug, 'Hey, John. Get out of my way!' I was poised over a fairly simple black at the time. I missed, and Dougie rolled back in. I wish people would show some consideration.

OTHER PLAYERS TALKING
DENNIS TAYLOR

Oh yes, I remember playing sticks with Alex. When he arrived in Blackburn I used to practise with him quite a bit. I actually met him in 1967, so I've known him longer than most of the others. He probably won't tell you this but I worked for a television company in those days and I used to ferry Alex about in the car. He's always messed about with his cues. As soon as he gets one he'll doctor it and cut a few inches off. I think he prefers a Burwat Champion. Alex hits the ball so much harder than anybody else that on

Dennis Taylor with family.

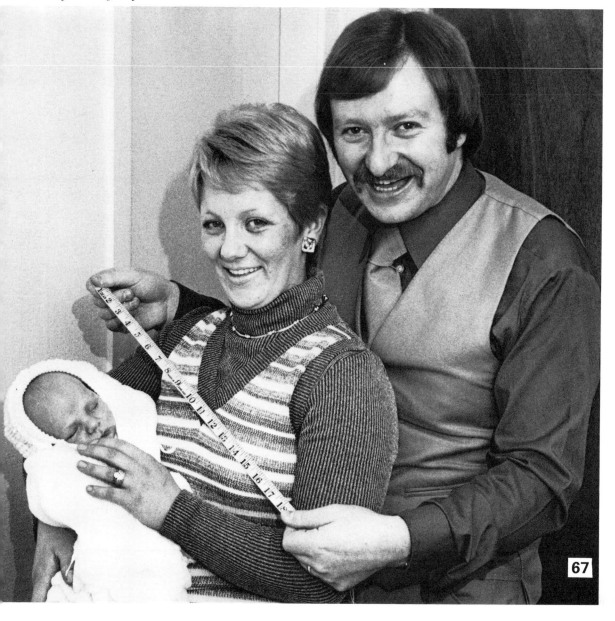

deep screw shots, if he miscues even slightly, he takes a lump out of his tip. He's a very, very good safety player, but the majority of the time he just has to have a go. Yes, he does take more risks. Some of the other players can play the shots he does, it's just that *they* wouldn't do it in a match. Nobody underestimates him as a positional player: I think everybody appreciates what a tremendous positional player he is as well as a tremendous potter. He loses position occasionally because he tries to get there in a way that's different from everybody else. Another player might content himself with a little screw shot, whereas Alex will hit the ball a lot harder, with a lot more side, off two or three cushions.

Dennis Taylor, with the 'perfect cue'.

Dennis Taylor

Dennis Taylor, with female companion.

OTHER PLAYERS TALKING
JACK REA

He has natural ability, it's as simple as that. When he beat me for my Irish Pro title he was a pure attacking player, willing to gamble on position. He'd no safety play then at all. Other than that, I doubt that his game has changed. I thought when he got married it might, but I don't think so now. It's natural ability, natural ball control. You should see him play table tennis! He's better at that than he is at darts. I believe he should have won the World Championship in 1980. I don't think, personally, that Thorburn is in the same class. But top level snooker is a matter of nerves, and who can best control them. It's the pressure that's killing Alex. It happens to us all as we approach victory: you can't think; you lose your confidence. You think the world is against you. You're afraid to go for your shots. Top level snooker is all about about pressure: the man who can control himself best, who can hold himself together, is the man who wins, and in 1980 it was Thorburn.

CLIFF THORBURN

concentrate more on making as many as he can when he gets in. I guess he's the best positional player in the world with his *style* of position. Nobody plays position like him. He was one of the first players to break out reds from potting the red, which is a very difficult thing to do. Most players, when they want to break out the pack, will do it off a colour, and they have to get a little bit lucky. Whereas Alex, when he's potting a red, will sometimes go into the pack and glance off and knock a couple of reds out and maintain his position on a coloured ball.

His use of side and screw is definitely different from other players: he doesn't hold the cue that tight, so the cue responds to his type of grip, because his hand is so loose. When you hold the cue light like he does, it's much easier to follow through, but it's a more difficult touch game, under pressure especially. But he's so talented that he can get away with it. I'm sure that if he could maybe tighten up his game a little bit, and get a bit 'old fashioned', he might be a better player, but Alex just lives mostly by response from the crowd, and I'm sure that he wouldn't want to play the game normally because he loves people clapping when he's playing. He said that he played to the crowd against me in the 1980 World Championship, but I don't think that's entirely fair, because *I* would say that I made him restless. At one time I tried to slow him down—slower than I played him in that final, and he does get very, very restless. The way that he plays he's never going to be the 'perfect' player, but he's going to be the most exciting, and 75 per cent of the people who play snooker probably identify with him more than anybody else.

Alex is underestimated as a safety player: he's as good as anybody in the world at playing safety shots and, like a lot of the top professionals, he's an offensive safety player—he's not interested in just hitting the cue ball down to the bottom of the table. But then you can only get *so* good playing safe anyway, because anyone who spends all his time practising safety shots won't be able to pot a ball when he gets the chance—that's the killer. I used to play more safeties than I do now, but I had to change. In order to beat somebody like Alex I just had to go for pots.

Potting? Well, Alex doesn't necessarily have the best cue action. But he's the only player there is who can play near as well as he does without actually keeping *still*. He has told me that at the point of impact he's all solid, and that it's as soon as the cue tip strikes the cue ball that he starts to move. But you see, it isn't—he does actually move his head and everything before he strikes the ball. Yet he's got so much ball sense—it's a natural gift to a certain extent. He's got more ball sense than anybody else, I would say. Lately he's been shortening his backswing as well, and he's very, very good around the pink and black, more so than before, but when you've got a short backswing, your long potting's going to be affected. His long potting isn't near as good as it used to be because he's trying to

OTHER PLAYERS TALKING
WILLIE THORNE

He goes for pots that nobody else would go for. That's the main difference. So when you play a safety shot yourself, you never know whether you're safe against him. You can never tell whether he's going to dig one out from somewhere, or when he's going to let fly. I don't think you could say its because of the crowds, because he plays like this even in practice. If his opponent is potting well, though, Alex seems to try and go one better—like he did against Steve in the UK final—going for shots and going for shots, though it was in a lost cause. I think he's better than he was in 1972, but then so is everybody else as well. Alex is one of the three or four best safety players in the *world*. And his temperament is perfect. His record over the past few years speaks for itself: you don't win the titles he's won and reach the finals he has without a superb temperament. Everybody else's record has been patchy; Alex has stayed in there since 1972: nobody else can say that, except maybe Reardon when he had his long winning spell. Technically he's just a phenomenon. He does everything wrong: his stance is square, he lifts his head, his arm's bent, he snatches at some of his shots. In fact, his delivery is the only thing that's right. Yet he can do what he does: it's amazing. Of all the pros, Alex would be about the last one you'd want to copy technically!

FITS
and
STARTS

I DEFENDED my Irish Professional title twice during 1978. The first challenger was Dennis Taylor. After the match, at the Ulster Hall, Belfast, Taylor told the *Belfast Telegraph*'s Ronnie Harper, 'It's like a bad dream,' and for him, it was. We had to play the Saturday evening games as an exhibition because by then I'd already beaten him 21–7. I was playing in front of my home crowd: they always bring out something special in me. Later in the year came Patsy Fagan, at the same venue, and I'm afraid it was like a bad dream for him as well. Fagan lost, 13–21. I've always defended my Irish title in fine style except for 1980, when Dennis Taylor beat me. I was sick on my sister Ann's porch that night. I just felt awful.

In February I won the Benson and Hedges Masters at the New London Theatre, Drury Lane. I won't say I was unstoppable. You could have stopped me with an elephant gun. But I meant to win. I beat Dennis Taylor in the quarters, 4–3—I think he was still feeling a bit demoralized from our Belfast meeting—and I buried Reardon in the semi, 5–1. I remember I played some very good snooker in that. I was two frames up in 20 minutes and I led 4–0 in 61 minutes. It would have been a lot faster but Ray takes a while to chalk his cue. He tried to slow the tempo down with a lot of sly safety in the fourth frame, but I was on song and the balls were running for me. I fluked a couple of snookers and that finished him off really. In the final, I beat Cliff Thorburn. I was 3–0 ahead but he came back to level and then take a 5–4 lead. In the 10th frame Cliff came unstuck. He led 40–5 but miscued on a long red and let smart Alex back in for 41. I led by 20 with only the pink and black on the table, but

Still smiling.

74

John Spencer says the reason I'm good with the rest is that my legs are short.

then I conceded 6 from a crafty snooker. Thorburn requested me to play again, and as you may already have noticed with me, this is never a good idea. I doubled the pink from the baulk cushion to the top pocket so fast, I think it may have frightened him. I won the last two frames I needed for the match and £3000. The score was 7–5.

The World Championships in 1978 had everything. They had the venue—the Crucible has been the favourite setting ever since—they had the prizemoney, and thanks to Nick Hunter's BBC team, they had the daily television coverage. The only thing they didn't have was the Hurricane, because I lost in the first round. It was that Patsy Fagan, coming back from the grave where I'd buried him in the Irish title match just previously. I don't know; maybe I was tired, or maybe I didn't take him as seriously as I

should have done. With an entertaining pink and black finish, I led 11–10 and then went two up with three to play. In the next frame a break of 66 took me to within a green of victory, but it stayed out. Fagan got back in, tied the frame, and potted the re-spotted black to creep up 11–12. He won the next frame on the black and a cliff-hanging decider on a colours clearance to the pink, to beat me 13–12. Edged me out, so he did. The tension was so fantastic towards the finish that they had to practically read the crowd the Riot Act, and a young fan of mine with a bone marrow disease, Tony Metcalf, collapsed with the shock of seeing me lose. I think there was a collection for him afterwards to pay his hotel for a couple of days, and they got him some spare tickets, otherwise he'd have had to go back to Barrow-in-Furness disappointed.

75

1978 was an eventful year all round. I lost the final of the Champion of Champions tournament at Wembley to Ray Reardon, 11–9, and I was quoted at the time as saying Reardon and I were really the only ones in it at the top of the game. It was just him and me, really. I made my fourth 'official' 147 in practice in Toronto. I should actually have made two on the trot, but the next frame I was down to the pink and black and instead of getting the rest I tried to stretch for it. I missed the pink, and I was perfect on the black as well. It was just carelessness.

At the Club Double Diamond in Caerphilly, I had a fight with Graham Miles. Graham's alright and we've always been mates, but he'd had all the run of the balls in this round robin thing and he beat me for the £500. As he stepped up to take the winner's cheque I think I may have said something like, 'You jammy bald b----!' or what have you, and he stuck one one me, so he did. It didn't connect, but it caused me to overbalance into the auditorium. Well, no matter how I may have antagonised him with the hair references, I don't think he should have done that in front of people, so afterwards I got him in the dressing room. We were separated by a couple of bouncers, and the pair of us fined £200. Funny really.

I was omitted from *Pot Black* once again for some misdemeanour, and I was also not among those invited to take part in some so-called 'World' Matchplay Championships, organised by Eddie Charlton and scheduled to take place in Melbourne the following March. Now, as I've said, my private life is my own business and nothing whatever to do with the playing of snooker at the table, where my behaviour has always been above reproach if you look back over the years. As for these Matchplay invitations: I should have thought the sponsors would have *wanted* a draw, and such an exciting player as myself. Of the first 13 players in the W.P.B.S.A. ranking list, I was the only one not invited. But there wasn't that much I could do, because I didn't really get the backing of my fellow-professionals in the W.P.B.S.A., who sanctioned the event and approved the word 'World' in the title. I'm sure I would rally round any one of them if I thought they were being unfairly treated, but there you are. As it happened, the gods were on my side anyway. Eddie's famous Matchplay

Left: Making the white ball talk.

At the World Professional Championships in 1976. Left to right: Ray Reardon, S. Pearson, Alex Stepney, myself, Paddy Roche, Gerry Daly.

Right: Prestatyn, 1977, the year I won Pontins Open. Lurking in the background are Tony Meo, John Pulman and John Spencer trying to grow a moustache.

Below: Ray Reardon, making the best of conditions at the C.N.E Centre tournament in Toronto, 1977. A neighbouring tent contained a dancing elephant.

Pontins Open winner, '77, from scratch qualifier, with Billy Kelly, John Williams and George Scott.

Champion of Champions, '77: the eventual winner sizing things up.

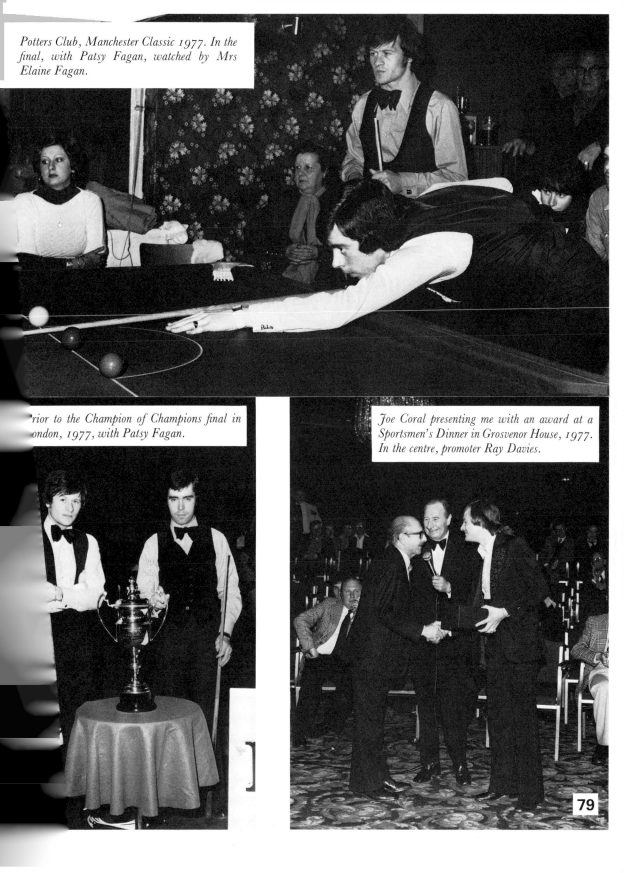

Potters Club, Manchester Classic 1977. In the final, with Patsy Fagan, watched by Mrs Elaine Fagan.

...rior to the Champion of Champions final in ...ondon, 1977, with Patsy Fagan.

Joe Coral presenting me with an award at a Sportsmen's Dinner in Grosvenor House, 1977. In the centre, promoter Ray Davies.

79

Left: Winning the Benson and Hedges Masters in 1978.

Below: Playing Dennis Taylor in the Benson and Hedges Masters, '78.

Above right: Dennis Taylor gets down to it. Benson and Hedges Masters, 1978.

In play at the Masters tournament, 1978: I beat Thorburn in the final.

At the Ulster Hall, Belfast in 1978, to defend my Irish Professional title v. Patsy Fagan.

Below: Having a look at Perrie Mans' daisy-chain as he wins the
Benson and Hedges Masters final at Wembley, 1979.

Championships never came off the following year, because the sponsors withdrew. The whole thing was described in *Snooker Scene* as a 'monumental shambles.' And of course, when March rolled around, I was booked up, whilst all the invited players were out of work.

At the start of '79 my cueing was off. I've a wasted muscle in my right knee, even though I walk a lot and I'm very active. It was sore at the beginning of that year. I should have thought you put your weight on both legs about equally playing snooker, but something was definitely taking the strain as I went out to Graham Miles in the semi-final of the Holsten Lager International in Slough. I had other things on my mind as well; personal problems hanging over me which were nobody's business but my own, but which found their way into big newspaper spreads as usual. I hate people gloating over me as though I were something to be bought in a shop. I'm not public property. Inevitably, these things creep into your line of thought when you're trying to concentrate at the table.

The Benson and Hedges Masters at Wembley Conference Centre looked like being a good tournament for me again that year. I rolled over Doug Mountjoy 5–1, but even more satisfying was a 5–2 victory over Mr Eddie Charlton, our World Matchplay Championships organizer, sporting a natty new hair transplant. I was 3–1 up at the interval, and after Eddie had taken a red and a blue, I stepped in and made a 132 clearance, with 14 reds, 11 blacks, 2 blues, a brown and all the colours. The feature of this clearance, which surpassed the previous record break of 97 for these championships set by E. Charlton in 1976, was my ingeniousness in dislodging reds from the pack. It was what you might call vintage Higgins, and I wasn't just playing to the galleries either. A poor first session against Perrie Mans in the final cost me that match, 8–4. I never really hit my stride till it was too late.

When Eddie Charlton withdrew from the Pontins Festival at Prestatyn he was replaced, not by me, but by an Australian, Ian Anderson. I was busy all year, though, as I never stop. One of my TV appearances was on *A Question of Sport*, in Emlyn Hughes' team with boxer Maurice Hope. Maurice didn't say an awful lot, but Emlyn and I share the same sense of humour.

I made another memorable century-break during the course of my third Irish title defence at the Ulster Hall, Belfast. I disabled Patsy Fagan 21–12, and the break came in the 30th frame. I'd potted two reds and a green before coming to the table for a 122 break in 2 minutes 45 seconds. The referee, Alf Shaw of Leeds, described it afterwards as 'sheer brilliance', and comments appeared in the snooker press at the time that there was little point in either Dennis Taylor or Patsy challenging me again for the Irish title while my margin of superiority was so great. It wasn't the 'fastest ever' break though—not by me. I've made a 110 break in 2 minutes 4 seconds, and if you speculate and stick a couple of balls on that, my striking rate would have to have been something like 130 or 140 in maybe 2½ minutes or 2 minutes 35 seconds.

Once again though, the World Championships were a disappointment for the Hurricane. In the first round I beat David Taylor, 13–5. In the quarter-final, Terry Griffiths (Llanelli) beat Alex Higgins (Belfast), 13–12. You may remember that match. I started out making back-to-back century-breaks in the second and third frames, and a 45 in the fourth. A third consecutive century was on the cards, and it would have been a record for the Championships, but I let Griffiths in and he compiled a winning clearance. I won all four of the remaining frames in that session, though. I was cruising, 6–2. On resumption Terry closed the gap to a single frame, 6–5; I opened it up again to three, 8–5, only for him to level in the evening session. So we started the next day all-square. He took the opener to lead 9–8; I accounted for the second with a 63 break, and it was nip-and-tuck like that until at the mid-session interval we stood at 10-all. Everyone will tell you that the key to the match was the 23rd frame, with the score 11–11, me leading 55–0 and in perfect position for the black. I missed that black, and it was my own fault, but that wasn't the key to the match, because I pulled back that frame to stand all-square again at 12–12. In the *final* frame, trying to pot a long red in the top pocket, I got a definite kick. It kept the ball out, and I was obliged to sit and watch Griffiths compile his 107 break to win the match. That was the key. There's nothing you can do about it, but it breaks your heart when it happens at such a crucial time.

(Terry Griffiths: I'll never forget his face afterwards. I'd just won the last frame of a very good match and I'd come over to shake his hand—and I wanted to cry for him. I'd just beaten him, you know; it was the biggest day of my life, but it was so pitiful to see his face.)

Left: Lynn, myself and a young fan at Potters Club, Manchester in 1979. Note the Fedora hat, which has since been given to a hospital patient.

Below: High class service at the Crown Bar, Belfast in 1979.

In Ireland for the Benson and Hedges Irish Masters.

On holiday in Tenerife in 1979 with friends Geoff, Helen and Barbara.

Cleaning the cue ball before I was banned from so doing. This was at the Benson and Hedges Masters at Wembley in 1979. The shirt is Chinese.

Revealing the Higgins gimpy knee, 1979.

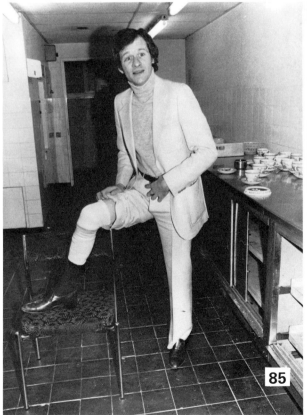

OTHER PLAYERS TALKING
JOHN VIRGO

It's difficult to isolate any one strength: he's got more natural ability than anyone I've ever seen playing the game. He plays almost purely on instinct—that's why he's able to size up situations on the table so fast. He reads the game very, very quickly, it's almost a sixth sense with him. When he's playing well, a technical weakness like bobbing his head up doesn't matter because when he *is* playing well his head is down, and

what he does afterwards is immaterial; the shot's been played. Besides, the most important technical aspect of any ball game is the follow-through. Alex has the best follow-through of anybody. In a game like snooker, you have time to think about a shot, so it could never depend entirely on reflexes. But the player who comes closest to reflex snooker is Alex.

I think he takes a lot more care over his shots than he used to. When he's on form his all-around game is a lot stronger than it was in 1972. In '72 he was just potting everything in sight. The only trouble is that when things go wrong now, and Alex gets into a corner, he tries to revert back. He's impatient. We haven't met in a championship match but I've watched him play percentage players and 'spoilers': eventually Alex will get fed up and have to go for it.

Left below: John Virgo, UK Champion.

The type of game that Alex plays is very open. If he's up against an opponent who's playing well, Alex will leave him chances, like he did against Steve Davis in the last UK Championship final. And you can't give another professional chances like that. But there are other advantages against Alex. The table stays relatively neat and tidy, whereas a safety player will manoeuvre the balls about and there's no set pattern. And then there's the time factor. Alex can go to the table and make an 80 break and it'll seem like no time at all; another sort of opponent might make 50 and you feel you've been out of the game for ages while he's been at the table. Alex has got this tremendous love of the game though. You feel he gets as much enjoyment out of clearing the colours as another pro might get out of a big break. That love of the game can be a disadvantage, because now he's so popular and gets so many bookings, it must get boring for him. I think that's why he's begun to struggle a bit—it's because his great love for snooker is on the wane. When I was an amateur Alex came in our club and played from 1pm to 1am, just for the pleasure of playing. He's the only pro who'll go to a venue and actually carry on playing all night if his performance didn't satisfy him. That's how much he's loved the game. But I don't think the pressures of the Wimbledon-style fortnight World Championship suit him. When he won it in '72, you had a chance to recover between matches. Now it builds up for two weeks, so he can't unwind.

OTHER PLAYERS TALKING
JIMMY WHITE

I would say, when Alex is playing well, he's the best potter I've ever seen. In fact, when he *is* playing well, he's the best at every type of game—potting, positional play, safety, everything. He does take risks—I think that's the only way he can play: he could never stand to quieten his game down. The reason he hasn't won the World Championship since '72 is that he *knows* the game so much that he expects to do it all in one shot. At times, yes, he does play to the galleries, but it's probably half-and-half, really. When he wants to play a larey shot, it's partly for the crowd, and partly for himself. I know he's not happy with his cues because he sits up till all hours fiddling about with them. I've seen him doing it: I fell asleep on the sofa in his house about two o'clock one morning while he was messing about doctoring one of his cues. But Alex is the best there is when he's playing well. He's the only snooker player that other players will actually go and watch. Including me. They might not admit it, but players will sneak to venues to see Alex.

Jimmy White, 4th from left. Centre, Tony Meo, bum-pinching.

Woods. 3rd from right, Tony Meo. 5th from right, Jimmy White.

Same scene.

OTHER PLAYERS TALKING
REX WILLIAMS

I think one of the strengths of Alex's game is safety play. I never thought that he could win the World Championship again after he won it in 1972 and I was nearly proved wrong last year: he played very good safety and I think had he not abandoned that type of game he would have beaten Cliff Thorburn. There are certain players—John Pulman at his best, Fred Davis at his best—who, if they weren't playing well and putting it together, could turn on the safety and play that type of game. Higgins can do that—because he's a very good player. I think his mind at times works in reverse to anyone else's. Shots that the normal player plays with one side, Higgins, for some reason, plays with the other side. And I often think, well this is strange, because these particular shots, we would find it very difficult to play with the side that he uses. He's a very, very good positional player. I watch him play at times and I think this fellow has no idea how to play the game and then other times I think

there's a touch of genius about him. I think he's got a good temperament. What amazes me is that he jumps all over the place, he throws his head, he throws his cue and does all sorts of peculiar things but really, he's a battler. When I played him in that semi-final in 1972, he doubled a pink into the corner pocket to win a frame. It's a shot that he probably wouldn't play these days— he knows too much about the game now—it was an inexperienced shot, the sort that an experienced player likes to see his opponent playing. But he kept on getting them *in* in that last session. He kept pulling off these shots that he shouldn't have been playing.

I don't think there's any doubt that he's lost confidence since 1972. I think it's all to do with pressure: it's very much easier to win the Championship than to hold on to it. And after Alex had won it, I believe he felt he had to keep proving himself. I don't think he had to, but I believe that's what he felt.

ALMOST THERE . . .

I N 1980 I won some, I lost some, I paid £400 in fines to the W.P.B.S.A., married Lynn, had a daughter Lauren, played golf, played Galaxians, played Graham Miles in a concrete stadium in Hong Kong, and missed winning the World Championship by whatever it takes for me to resist the crowd.

I started out buzzing. In the first two months of

The dashing bridegroom with Best Man Geoff Lomas outside Winslowe Reformed Church, January 5th, 1980.

1980 I played in six tournaments. I lost in the final of the Wilsons Classic in Manchester, won the Padmore/Super Crystalate at West Bromwich, lost in the final of the Benson and Hedges Masters at Wembley, and lost in the semi-final of the Irish Masters in Dublin. Then I won the Tolly Cobbold at Ipswich and the new British Gold Cup at Derby. People say 'Alex Higgins is highly strung. He gets into arguments, starts trouble, brings the game into disrepute.' Well, let me give you an example of my schedule. In the Gold Cup I lost to Dennis Taylor 2–1, breaking two tips, beat Terry Griffiths 3–0 with a 135 total clearance and a 14-red 134 clearance in successive frames, tore up to Ipswich, beat Dennis Taylor 5–4 in the final of the Tolly Cobbold, had a flaming row about a refereeing decision, finished the match after midnight, travelled through the night to Derby, arrived at 6 am, slept for 2½ hours, played my Gold Cup semi-final against Tony Meo at 11 am, beat him 4–0, slept for an hour in the afternoon and beat Reardon 5–1 in the evening final for £4000. Now, after a few days of this, you are burnt out. You do not wish to speak to Anglia Television. You do not wish to be grilled by assorted news men about 'incidents', or about your private life. All you wish, really, is for a bit of peace.

At the Wilsons Classic, at the New Century Hall, Manchester, I lost 3–4 in the final to John Spencer, and yes, there was an 'incident'. In the third frame I potted the yellow at speed and with a lot of screw to bring it back up the table. The yellow and the cue ball had been only a few inches apart, and this combination of circumstances inspired the referee, Jim Thorpe, to rule a push stroke. Jim Thorpe had ruled a push stroke against me, you may recall, in the 1974 World Championship quarter-final against Fred Davis which annoyed me some-what. Now here he was, at it again. Spencer was

With Richard Puttock in Treviscoe, March 1980.

quoted as saying there was indeed 'something odd' about the way the cue ball 'started to travel sideways before coming back'. Well, the reason it went sideways was because the pot was off straight and I used left-hand side. In my view I *couldn't* have pushed the ball: it's just that Jim Thorpe had made a wrong decision against me as I believe he did before. He wouldn't reverse it then, and he wouldn't reverse it now. That's what I thought, anyway, and that's what I said, in no uncertain terms.

Another refereeing decision that made me very annoyed was at the Tolly Cobbold in Ipswich, in the fifth frame of the final between myself and Dennis Taylor. I was snookered and obliged to swerve, and the black and the red were close together. Foul, says referee Nobby Clarke. I thought, bloody hell, I hit the red as clear as day. Foul, he says, for hitting the black. Then, to make matters ten times worse, about two shots later there was a free ball given against me when it shouldn't have been, and I thought well, this is getting too much. I think Dennis was about four or

five feet away from me at the time and it wasn't directed specifically at him, but I said, half under my breath, 'Bloody cheats!' I never meant any harm but I was so exasperated. Well, Dennis and Nobby reported me to the W.P.B.S.A. for that. As it turned out, the tournament was televised, and a lot of viewers wrote into *Points East* about the incident where I was supposed to have hit the black. They replayed the shot in slow motion, and what do I hit? The red. Yet I was fined £200 for that little lot.

If I commit a foul in a match, whether I'm playing for £50,000 or 50p, I will always call it. If the referee hasn't seen it, I will call the shot on myself and penalize myself. I have always done this, and the majority of referees know it, and the majority of my opponents will admit it. Opponents who are willing to stand by and see me fouled by the referee unfairly and yet say nothing, must be pretty desperate to beat me by any means they can. I must put them under a lot of pressure, for them to want to score off me like that. I have suffered some diabolical refereeing decisions,

The man in the Fedora hat. With Kirk Stevens and Lynn at Sheffield Crucible Theatre for the 1980 Embassy World Championships.

and been the only one on my side. It seems I am the one player who never has anything reversed in his favour. It may be that I move too fast for some refs to keep an eye on: you generally find that referees get in the way of players anyway, even those that don't move particularly fast. They start in the wrong place, they pick balls out of the pockets when they shouldn't do, they move in the players' line of vision. The best referee is the one you never see, and there are very few of those about.

One referee I *did* see recently was John Williams. I saw him, in the final of the 1980 Coral UK Championships, retrieve the pink in the middle of Steve Davis's break in the 12th frame, and instead of re-spotting the pink, pick up the cue ball and place it carefully on the pink spot. Realizing his mistake, he then proceeded to hazard a guess as to where the white was, and put it back on the table. I didn't think he had any right to do that, but they wouldn't even allow me a second opinion.

I know refs are only human and we all make mistakes. But I think referees are generally *more* susceptible to making mistakes than the players, because we professionals know the game inside out. They don't. There isn't what *I* would call a professional referee in the game. I reckon that's why there are so many mistakes. And that's why I flare up when I've been outrageously treated. I was given two maximum fines by the W.P.B.S.A. during 1980 for 'using abusive language to referees' and 'bringing the game into disrepute'. I'm not bringing the game into disrepute. It's my livelihood. And when a refereeing decision or anything else affects my livelihood, I think I've every right to speak my mind.

The W.P.B.S.A. also ruled that I was to be penalized in future for removing my tie, and for licking the cue ball between frames. First of all, in regard to the tie, I get a rash on my neck through the heat and the sweat and the tension, and I've submitted a doctor's note to that effect which has

Househunting, 1979.

Bride and groom.

Bridegroom with Mum and Dad.

Below: Two pictures: left to right: John Hough, Lynn's brother, Best Man Geoff Lomas, myself and journalist friend John Dee.

...ueing up at our wedding.

97

Cueing up at our wedding outside Winslowe Reformed Church, January 5th, 1980. Mrs Lynn Higgins.

Right: Bride and groom.

I do practise occasionally. Prior to the Embassy World Championships at the Crucible Theatre, Sheffield, 1980.

been accepted by the Players' Association. But I think, in any sport, you should have unrestricted freedom of movement. A lot of players who don't actually remove their ties still loosen them on occasions, for that reason. I think it's fine to wear a bow tie for prize-giving ceremonies, or when you're being presented to the audience or the dignitaries. But then when you get down to play, it's like a footballer taking off his tracksuit. You don't want to be constricted around the throat when you're playing under pressure.

As regards licking the cue ball: you may know that in snooker we get a lot of what we call 'kicks'—occasions when the balls don't throw true. I think my cleaning the white ball helps to prevent kicks not only for me, but for my opponent as well. A lot of the time the referees tend to forget to clean the balls, so I got into the habit of religiously picking up the white as soon as it stopped rolling at the end of a frame, and giving it a little lick. I carried two handkerchiefs: one for my nose obviously, and a clean one for the ball, because

when you ask for a damp cloth at a tournament you have to spend half your time wringing out what they give you. I'm not doing any harm licking the cue ball. Nobody *else* is going to lick it, so they're not likely to catch anything. A professional golfer cleans his golf ball. A professional bowler puts spit on a cricket ball for adhesion, and to bring up the shine. Yet a professional snooker player trying to clean the most important ball on the table gets reprimanded by the Players Association. It doesn't make a lot of sense.

1980 was a mixed blessing for me in many ways. I won several tournaments, including the Super Crystalate International, with flu and an ear infection; I won the Pontins Professional at Camber Sands; and I helped Joe Brown win the Pro-Celebrity trophy, though I was full of a cold the whole time and a doctor from Leeds Infirmary dosed me up with antibiotics. Joe and I stopped Dennis Taylor's run in that, as he'd already won it two years on the trot. I was sick to my stomach when I lost my Irish Professional title to Dennis 21–15 at the Ulster Hall, and I was pretty damn sick about losing the Masters final 9–5 to Terry Griffiths at Wembley, after I'd stormed through the earlier rounds beating Fred Davis 5–1, Perrie Mans 5–1 and Ray Reardon 5–2 in the semi.

Another final I reached in 1980 was the Coral UK Professional Championship at Preston. To reach the last eight I'd upset Willie Thorne 9–7 with the help of a 134 total clearance and an Irish fluke in the final frame, and I'd beaten Fred 9–6 in the quarters, after the old devil had fought back from 3–8 down with an amazing snooker, weaseling the cue ball behind the black with only the pink and black remaining. I believe it was at that point that I remarked to Fred, 'Why don't you just lay down and die?' though Fred knows I don't mean a thing by it and we held hands at the post-match TV interview. In the semi it was Reardon, whom I outsnookered in the finish 9–7, and in the final it was ginger Steve Davis, who caught me napping, I'm afraid, 16–6 for the £6000 first prize. I played about thirty percent of my game, and he played a hundred percent of his, which was what

inspired Corals to make him their 5–1 favourite for the World Championships 1981.

But my biggest disappointment by far in 1980 was losing the World Championship final to Cliff Thorburn 18–16. It was a magnificent final, one that people will remember, and it attracted a record TV viewing audience of 14.5 million. I'd had the worst of the draw, as usual. A very tight first-round match against Tony Meo playing out of his skin, which I won 10–9, a 13–6 victory over Perrie Mans, a 13–9 win over Steve Davis in the quarter-final, in which Davis compiled a 136 total clearance in the first session, and a tense 16–13 win over Kirk Stevens, who was within striking distance of me at 12–14 and smacking in long pots to prove it.

But it's the final that makes you or breaks you. I really felt 1980 might be my year another Year of the Hurricane, so to speak. I was on my game in that final. But I wanted to win it in style, I wanted to do it the flamboyant way. I led 5–1, 6–2 and 9–5 before losing my self-restraint. I was lucky it didn't turn out worse, actually, because there were four games when

In play in casual attire at the Canadian Open, 1980.

Right: Looking appropriately concerned in the final of the Coral UK Championship in 1980, where Steve Davis beat me.

Above: Sartorial elegance.

I was 50 in front and let Cliff back in, and there wasn't a colour on the cushion to save me. It's always harder to build up a 50 break at the beginning than it is to do it at the end of a frame when you've got three reds, three blacks and all the colours on their spots. Thorburn won the last four frames of that evening session to start afresh the next day all-square. Even when we stood level at 9–all, I thought I could haul him in. He led by two frames; I caught back up. He led by one frame; I caught back up. But Thorburn is a grinder. He grinds you hard, and I suppose by 12–12 the run of the balls was beginning to desert me. I think it's my own fault I lost. As I'm getting older, I'm disciplining myself more, keeping myself under control. In 1980 I was only one or two sessions of disciplined safety play short. Just a couple of sessions. But that's how I lost the Championship. Playing to the crowds, trying to do it the flash way.

Lynn, with Jimmy White.

Myself and Jimmy White.

With manager Del Simmons waiting to go over Niagara Falls in a barrel.

...way from the table. Left to right: Dennis Taylor, ...um, Ray Reardon, Lynn, ...ster Jean.

105

With footballer Gerry Daly, Patsy Fagan, footballer Dunne and John Virgo.

Looking over Niagara Falls.

Sister Jean with Rod Stewart look-alike.

With my aunt Jean.

Myself and Mrs Higgins.

Sister Jean with wife Lynn. Note the uncanny resemblance.

108

Without a visa, the US Immigration Department wouldn't let even the Hurricane in. (Two pictures.)

Left: Myself with 'afro' (and Patsy Fagan).

Above: 'He stuck one on me, so he did'.

Right: Presenting a cheque to Patsy Fagan's other half, Elaine.

OTHER PLAYERS TALKING
GRAHAM MILES

Is he unusual as a positional player? Well, at times I think he tries to make the shot appear a little more difficult than it is, by using extremes of side and screw. It's one of his habits when things are going well. On occasions he tries these spectacular shots that sometimes come off and sometimes don't, but I don't think it's 'playing to the galleries'—I think that's nonsense, myself. I think he appreciates the element of danger, and so does his opponent. It must be understood that he's not the only player who can produce these shots: in a match you can play a shot one day and you'll get it nine times out of ten, and another day you can't get anywhere near the bloody thing. Snooker's a funny game. It doesn't matter how good you are, your game can vary, and nobody can ever exactly pinpoint why it happens. You can be very good, or you can be rubbish. It all depends. Alex is more of a potter than a positional player. His potting is what mesmerizes audiences. But he does sometimes make the shot a little bit harder than it needed to be. Provided these magnificent shots come off, he's alright, and it's very attractive to watch, but it does make him a beatable commodity, because he'll take a chance. He plays a lot of forcing type shots, which means he gets his share of flukes.

Alex is highly-strung, character-wise. He has a nervous disposition, but he's certainly got match temperament because he's won a lot of matches under pressure. I think his run in the World Championships could perhaps have been better, but then you have to remember Alex is the only player who travels around like he does. He must be putting in more hours a day travelling than just about anyone. Yet he comes up with these really outstanding performances. A lot of people, if they had to travel about like he does, wouldn't be able to pick up a cue.

Graham Miles, breaking off against John Spencer.

Dennis Taylor (left) and Terry Griffiths.

OTHER PLAYERS TALKING
JIM WYCH

There's absolutely no doubt about it: when he's right, no one can really play with him. He's a fantastic potter. He's capable of making just about anything on the table and its probably his patience that people have to rely on giving out. If he ever keeps his patience and decides to wait for balls, he's got to be one of the most naturally talented players in the world, without a doubt. I don't think he really works on his game as much as some people do. I can believe that he doesn't practise—he's a very natural player. He has a tendency to speed the game up, as well, and his rhythm can break up the rhythm of his opponents at times. He's a considerably good clutch player: Alex's style of play in the clutch can be very effective, because he's so unpredictable. You don't know what he's going to do at any given time, so there are occasions when you don't even want to let him *see* a ball. He'll continually *make* low percentage shots, where another player wouldn't even consider such a shot, and he'll come out of it and play a deep screw shot or something to get on a colour where 90 per cent of the professionals in the game wouldn't

have the capabilities to get there. Positionally, when he's right, it's just pretty to watch. Players are always talking about themselves being 'right', being on their game, but Alex has got more shots and more ability when he's on his game than a good percentage of the professionals. I know he showed me some absolutely fantastic safety play in the World Championships. I always knew what kind of a potter he was, but he showed me that he could play safe like no one else in the world when he wants to. There were spots in the World Championships where some of the safeties he played were brilliant. I would have liked to have left anyone in the game in the spots that he was in, and let them try to get out of it the way he did. He's just so unpredictable, and that's part of his attack. Why hasn't he won the title since '72? Well, I would have to go along with a few of the other players and say possibly it's his life-style: I don't know whether he really takes care of himself, and with the style of snooker that there is now, you have an awful lot of younger players coming into the game that are not only good, but offensively minded as well.

Dennis Taylor (left) and Steve Davis.

Steve Davis (left) and Terry Griffiths at a challenge match.

Kirk Stevens pointing out John Virgo was late for the match in the Coral UK Championships. John won, though.

FUTURE HIGGINS

I BELIEVE I'll win the World Championship again, if not in 1981, sooner or later. Ideally you need a month off to prepare for a world title bid and with the heavy schedule I've had for so long, I think my mind's rejecting the game. I need to escape to the golf course occasionally, or the Space Invaders controls. I need a rest, so I can come back fresh to the table. Still, I nearly won the title in 1980. *With* my heavy schedule. With the trains and boats and planes, with no time or inspiration to practise, and without a cue I half-believed in. I was just a couple of sessions short on self-restraint, that's all. What's more, I won the 1981 Benson and Hedges Masters, beating Terry Griffiths 9–6 in the final and actually having a refereeing decision reversed in my favour by John Smyth, so things are definitely looking up.

It's very hard to get yourself ready for two particular weeks of the year. It's difficult to be in the right frame of mind in the right place at the right time. So I've been missing out in the World Championships. But when I was a little kid, marking for all and sundry in the Jampot, I went for years without winning anything. To eventually beat those grown men that continually fleeced me of my bits of pocket money and never made any allowances for the fact that I was just a little kid—it took so much perseverance, so much courage and belief in myself, that I'll never lose those qualities now, just because of a few setbacks in the World Championships. Those years taught me temperament. They taught me you've got to believe in yourself and your abilities. It's the same for anybody.

Of course, it's no good having a wonderful temperament without being able to play well. Fortunately I had the talent. It had to be brought out, by hours and weeks and years of constant practice and dedication to the game: it wasn't just a case of picking up a cue and smacking in record breaks with my natural flair. But I did have the flair, and I knew it. At the moment, I may not be able to show my talent to best advantage because I haven't the necessary confidence in a cue. I'm using a heavier cue than in my early days, and I'm experimenting. My cue has just been re-butted but still doesn't feel right. I'll just have to keep searching till I find the right one. When I do, I'll know as soon as I pick it up, as soon as I hit a ball with it. Then you'll see potting. My *position* has always been second to none. Nobody can make a white ball talk the way I can, but my cue action has gone off a bit. There must be an awful lot of talent still there for me to have stayed at the top of the game as I have done, without the right cue.

In my new house, when I get it, I'll have my own table installed, like I say, so I can play for an hour, watch TV for an hour, play more snooker, have a couple of drinks, invite people in that *I* want to play with—and all without any hassle. Because no matter where I go these days up and down the country, whether it's to billiard halls or labour or conservative clubs, I'm always pestered; I'm never free to just get on and practise. You can't enjoy the game if you're being hassled. People want to buy you drinks, they put things on the table for you to sign, they ask questions, they follow you about. I appreciate their attention, I really do—*nobody* has the reputation for crowd-pleasing that I have—but sometimes you need peace and quiet. Sometimes you need privacy to concentrate, and just to be left alone. With a table in my own home, I can play in good conditions; I can practise secretly, so to speak, and enjoy the game that much better. It gives you freedom to do what you feel like doing. Make centuries. Have the video on. Have boxing on.

I love boxing. I'm a real fight fan. I never missed a telecast of an Ali fight. I thought nothing of travelling from Grimsby to Nottingham to catch a closed circuit transmission. I went down to Southampton and booked into a hotel at about six in the evening, and I'd been up to my room to shave and change, and I asked the receptionist to check up with ABC or whoever was doing the closed circuit Ali fight in the area that evening. She said, Oh, they're not showing it in Southampton. Not showing it in Southampton?!? Well, I said, in that case I shall have to pay a cancellation fee. So I packed my bags and played my exhibition: oddly enough that particular night I made three century breaks, and somebody had said we'll give you a bottle of champagne if you make a hundred. I said not to worry about the champagne, but I'd like a bottle of vodka. So I ended up with three bottles of vodka, three bottles of tonic, an opener and a glass, and I proceeded to catch the last train to London from Southampton. Over to Leicester Square I went, and there I was for the night, drinking with Harry Carpenter and telling him he should have stuck to gardening and what have you, watching the Ali fight. I'd travel to the ends of the earth to see Ali. I tried to arrange to make the trip to Vegas for his last fight, but I was booked and I couldn't go. I'm glad now, because I'd have seen him degraded and humiliated, and I'd have felt that way too. I was in Ireland on the night, as it happened, and we picked up the fight on the radio in Dutch or German or something. I was in tears when Ali lost. Apart from Lester Piggott and Georgie Best, he was the only guy I ever really looked up to. People have criticised me in the past for behaving like the Ali of snooker. Well that's OK with me. Ali is in a class of his own. He is supreme—the all-time greatest.

Criticism over the years doesn't bother me. I don't care what all the fuddy-duddies say about me, because I put the game on the map. I don't think any of the younger players in snooker today would match up to Spencer, Reardon and myself at our best. I'm bound to say that, but I don't think they would. The younger players have been helped, for a start, by the fact that they've got an easier ball—they've gone straight into using these new Super Crystalate balls without having to make any transition. I won the World Championship with the old ball. So did Spencer and Reardon. We had genuine power play with the heavier ball, and the readjustment for us wasn't easy. You had to change your style to control the amount of power you used. The new breed of snooker players never had to make that transition like we did. You go back eight years and Tony Meo was

just 13. Jimmy White was 10.

Who are the three best players in the world over the last decade? In order: well, I have to put myself first because I'm not modest. Probably John Spencer is second. And Ray Reardon third. I think Spencer would still be a great player but for the breaking of his cue. When I was at my peak and Spencer was at his, we had more in common with each other than we had with Reardon. Ray was more or less *always* a safety player, though he could make his 70s and 80s as well. But he didn't change. For Spencer and myself, more depended on super talent for potting the balls. So whilst Reardon kept basically the same game, Spencer and I had our cues broken and had to reconcile ourselves to the fact that our potting was gradually going off. I think that's when Reardon came into his own. Of course, the game has changed: when I beat Spencer for the world title, you played a couple of safety shots to get in, but now you have to play long bouts of safety. Reardon may have had cue problems himself this past couple of years, but that trend towards safety can't have done him any harm either. Apart from maybe Charlton, Spencer and I were the only ones to threaten his supremacy. And of course, Reardon had the same cue for years.

I was a major force in bringing snooker out from the shadows. *Pot Black* made it fit into a television screen, but I was the one that made it a spectator sport, an entertainment. If I hadn't started the ball rolling like that, I doubt that you'd have the young boys in the game that there are now, because most of them were inspired by Alex Higgins. Maybe not in style, because technically I'm almost impossible to imitate, but certainly in spirit. The older players these days have accepted that the younger generation aren't just a passing phase in the game any more— that they're here to stay. So instead of hindering them, and criticising them, and trying to close the shop door in their faces like they did when *I* was 22, they're trying to help them. I myself would always help younger players in any way I can, giving them any advice I could, because I know how tough it is when you're starting out in the game. I think they've all benefited from my experience, in that respect. I don't think there's the same suspicion and fear in snooker about these younger players that there was about me. I don't think people are frightened of young guys like Kirk Stevens, perhaps because they don't have the sort of personality I had, or the charisma either. I think people want to help them

Myself, Steve Davis and Patsy Fagan with all the Lucania men.

rather than hurt them.

I happened before my time in my sport, like George Best in football. I think Best and I have more in common than just being Irish. Our careers developed along similar lines, though of course Best is in the shadows now. I've only met the guy half a dozen times, but I've always admired him. People were jealous of his talent like they were of mine. They envied and resented his lifestyle, like they did mine. Yet the same type of player coming along today would be given the star treatment—cosseted and looked after. They're paying a couple of million now for people who couldn't have wiped Bestie's boots. And they're rhapsodizing over young snooker players I'd have buried alive when I was a kid.

I don't know what the future holds for me. I'm a family man now. I couldn't tell you what effect that'll have—I don't know. I love kids. My little Lauren looks just like me. She was five weeks premature and only tiny, but she has the Higgins expressions, just like me at the table. People where I come from have close-

knit families, and mine is no exception. My family has stuck by me all along. My sister Ann has more than once hopped into a taxi with cue tips for me, things like that. And my parents moved to Accrington just to see that I got a decent meal occasionally when I was living there. My grandmother died when she was only 34, so my Mum had to bring up the family, and she's what you might call a fighter, a real character, a tower of strength. She's had her hands full sometimes with us. Like the time she'd saved up a few pounds in amongst some papers, and we were moving house or something, and my Dad tore the lot up and threw it on the fire, tidy like. People talk about me dicing with death on the snooker table, but my Mum does it in real life. Once she fell down a manhole. Another occasion, in Australia, she was a bit unfamiliar with the way the traffic comes from all directions out there and she stepped off the pavement in front of a

Right: Getting ready to tee off at Wentworth. I drove the 12th 300 yards that afternoon.

WENTWORTH CLUB

WEST COURSE

| YARDS
471
METRES
430 | HOLE
1 | PAR
4
STROKE
4 |

FAIRCLOUGH
FOR BRIDGES AND MOTORWAYS

125

juggernaut. A man standing on the kerb fainted with shock. My Mum's a great lady, a surviver, like me.

In addition to being fond of children, I'm also keen on animals: horses, cats, you name it. As kids we always had animals in the house. My Mum's got a little fat black and white dog called Boo, and a fawn Persian called Benjy. We had another Persian by the name of Robin, that attacked Perrie Mans. Perrie is a pigeon fancier, so perhaps that had something to do with it. Lynn and I were giving Mans a lift in our Renault to Manchester, and for some reason we had to have Robin in the car as well, and he was down between my feet at the front, quite snug. Now, Perrie, being a pigeon fancier and what have you, was a bit suspicious of our Robin and a bit nervous of him in a confined space such as a car, because this cat was a big bully and liable to tear the place up. Perrie was also edgy about the speed Lynn was driving, which was about 90 miles an hour—I don't think they go all that quick in South Africa. Anyway Robin sat there good as gold—he was only 11 months, but he was an enormous great fluffy thing, like a lion. Suddenly though, just as we turned a corner, I think I may have put the car heater on for Perrie's benefit in the back, and out flew Robin—ping!—straight at Perrie Mans. I think it may have been pidgin English he was talking at the time. Scared the daylights out of him.

I'm fond of horses and still ride occasionally. I think referee John Smyth's seen me on horseback once. I'm at home amongst the racing fraternity and some of my friends are jockeys and ex-jockeys. One pal of mine, Dezzie Cavanagh, runs a taxi service with Oliver Reed's son, Mark, down in Dorking. They always make me welcome; Dezzie's about fifty now, but he used to be a jockey too. He hasn't got any horses these days but he does have a dog, a fat labrador called Murphy, that wears glasses, wears a hat, and smokes the occasional cigarette. Dezzie's a character, and if he's watching me play snooker he usually has a few words to say about my opponents. Ray Reardon and I were doing an exhibition at some ultra-smart club in Camberley a while back and Dezzie sat on the special guest table informing people that Reardon looks like Dracula. You can't take him anywhere.

I have a lot of friends scattered about the country that I see when I'm on the road. I'm always on the road. I'd like to get into the position where I could just play a few exhibitions and concentrate on tournaments, but I'm not financially sound enough to do that. Hopefully, in the near future, I shall be able to afford a schedule like that, to give myself a chance. I need a routine where I can practise, in between travelling from pillar to post, to get myself cueing properly. A major factor is that I don't drive a car. It must be a lot easier, if you're off to a venue for a week, to be able to stick your suitcase in the boot, and your cue in the back, instead of having to carry the rotten thing all over the place, rushing for trains, rushing for planes and taxis and in and out of hotels. Some people say I drink too much, but look at my figure. I'm ten stone four. There's not an ounce of fat on me; I'm too active. Rushing for trains did that.

How long can I go on at this pace? Oh, indefinitely. I'm a whiz kid, and flamboyance will never die. I've made a 100 break in 2 mins. 4 seconds; when I'm cruising I can knock in a 100 break in three or four minutes, no problem. I've potted every ball on the table several times in under six minutes. I've made 12 maximums. With Spencer, I'm the only player to have compiled four centuries in successive frames. I've made over 10,000 centuries—it's probably approaching 11,000 now, but I've stopped counting because it became an everyday occurance. Every time I play, whether it's in practice or a tournament or exhibition, I expect to make a century break. When you're just starting out in the game, you get a charge out of a 100. It's a great feeling for you. Then there's your first 20 hundreds, or your first 100 hundreds, or your first thousand. But after that, it becomes routine. I don't get a charge out of a hundred nowadays. I get my thrills out of winning tournaments.

I'd like to win the World Championship again. I'd be super-dedicated. Missing out on the World Championships has been a big disappointment for me, but then I've been hurt before, and I've been disappointed before. I'll bounce back. Every year is a fresh year! You break the balls, and start all over again. My opponents are having their say about me in this book, but I'll tell you what—they'll be feeling the Hurricane blowing about their ears for many years to come yet, and I bet not one of them relishes the prospect. I may do other things these days: I may play golf and Galaxians, and you may even see me on *Top of the Pops* when they release a single I've recorded, called *147*, but basically, my game is snooker; always has been, always will be. And soon, the Year of the Hurricane will roll round again.

WENTWORTH CLUB
WEST COURSE

YARDS	HOLE	PAR
471	**1**	4
METRES		STROKE
430		4

FAIRCLOUGH
FOR BRIDGES AND MOTORWAYS

A.H.

Tables tighten every year. Refs are getting mean.
Long reds get longer, seeming to recede
like sunsets on the distant cush:
I used to pot them clean.
I knew weak spots they had, and they knew me—
one shot was usually enough:
the rustle of that string bag underneath,
a quick death, and the hunter home for tea.
I hardly felt my cue—it was my arm—
I scarcely looked on it as wood.
It seemed to whistle when I was on song:
the two tunes were the self same melody
and never a note wrong.
I whipped the crowds behind me—they were mine
like the Pied Piper dancing through the town
crying and laughing all at the same time
and out of the corner of my eye,
I'd see them, when I won, dance up and down.
But now the tables tighten every year,
the lights are harsher, snooker's on the wane.
I've seen it growing grey before my eyes
and bowing over like a man in pain

from heartache at the wins all snatched away,
the kicks he bore without complaint, the shame
and tension of the black that made him faint
and shrivel like a moth against a flame.
I've seen my game grow weary all these years,
learning the hard way—safety first and last:
you can't allow a pro an opening—
he'll kill you if he can, as you would him—
we clench each other with an iron grasp—
our jaws are set tight like the tables grim—
for every ball there's a fierce bargaining.
And through it all, I've learned to play the part
as clinically and cold as any man:
to grit my teeth and hide away my heart
and all the flair that made me what I am.
But sometimes when the house is full, sometimes
I hear a sound like the wind, and through my mind
there sails the magic of the coloured balls
and long reds like a matador's rich blood—
it takes me like a river in full flood
and bursts the banks of all these petty rules.
And then I hear my song without a name
and go back to the crowd from whence I came.

A.P.